YOUR DAUGHTER

The Girls' Schools Association

The Friday Project
An imprint of HarperCollins*Publishers*
77–85 Fulham Palace Road
Hammersmith
London W6 8JB

www.thefridayproject.co.uk
www.harpercollins.co.uk

This edition published by The Friday Project 2011

2

A catalogue record for this book is available from the British Library

ISBN 978-0-00-737122-8

'Cat's Eye' by Margaret Atwood, 1988, 1989, 1990, 1992, 1993, 1994, 1996, 1997,
2007, 2008, 2009. Reproduced with kind permission of Bloomsbury Publishing.

Set in Minion by Palimpsest Book Production Limited,
Falkirk, Stirlingshire
Printed and bound in Great Britain by Clays Ltd, St Ives plc

Mixed Sources
Product group from well-managed
forests and other controlled sources
www.fsc.org Cert no. SW-COC-001806
© 1996 Forest Stewardship Council
FSC

FSC is a non-profit international organisation established
to promote the responsible management of the world's forests.
Products carrying the FSC label are independently certified
to assure consumers that they come from forests that are managed
to meet the social, economic and ecological needs
of present and future generations.

Find out more about HarperCollins and the environment at
www.harpercollins.co.uk/green

Contents

Introduction

Sugar and spice and all things nice, or moods, malice and meanness? Bringing up a daughter in the twenty-first century can be a lonely and daunting prospect. But whether you are consoling a 6-year-old who has fallen out with her best friend, or discussing the debatable merits of body piercing with a truculent teen, help is now at hand from the specialists.

The heads and staff of around 200 leading girls' schools in the UK have come together in a unique collaboration to share their combined insights and wisdom on everything about educating and raising girls. Hundreds of thousands of girls passing through their care each year means there's not much these experts don't know about dealing with girls – and there's certainly nothing your daughter might do that would surprise them!

Your Daughter offers you the best advice from the popular MyDaughter website (www.MyDaughter.co.uk). So whether or not you send your daughter to a girls' school, *Your Daughter* gives you access to a wealth of practical information and advice based on real experience from trusted professionals.

Watching and guiding your daughter as she blossoms into a young woman with her own opinions, thoughts and moral code can be both terrifying and exciting. *Your Daughter* aims to help you along the way. For the latest advice and information visit www.MyDaughter.co.uk.

Sheila Cooper
Executive Director
Girls' Schools Association

Relationships

Families raise children but they are not the only source of influence or support. Particularly for girls, friends are crucial to happiness and sense of self-worth. Your daughter will be totally reliant on you in her early years. Together with her extended family, be they aunts, uncles and grandparents or step-families, you will nurture, guide and support her. She will find her friends in her neighbourhood and her school, through her hobbies and interests. A warm, loving network is the foundation on which your daughter will grow and by which she will be shaped. She will take her role models from those closest to her as she grows until she begins to look wider afield. The overwhelming majority of girls say that their mothers are their most influential role models. This is a great tribute but with it comes a huge responsibility – to set the best possible example, to guide and direct, to communicate and explain. As she matures your daughter will also be greatly influenced by her teachers and, above all, by her peers. The media will also have an effect, one which you will probably want to moderate by discussing with her those aspects which you consider admirable . . . and those you don't. It will not always be plain sailing. Everyone has to deal with disappointment and loss, with failure and heartache. At these times your daughter will rely on her relationships, with you and with others, to help her cope and to help her understand.

Family Relationships

The relationship between parents and their daughters can either be one of great stress and anguish throughout your daughter's teenage years or it can be one of growing respect and developing friendship, as you both move from the parent-child relationship to the more sophisticated relationship of parent-adult. Watching your daughter blossoming into a young adult, who has her own feelings, thoughts, actions and values, is both daunting and exciting to a parent, but it is important to let her fly and to trust her. At the core of all relationships, especially the parent/daughter one, is open and honest communication. It is crucial to keep the channels of communication open at all times with the aim of developing a long term relationship based on mutual trust.

The importance of family

Girls' relationships are typically far more complex than those of boys. In general, girls:

- talk more, and unconsciously pass all their thoughts through a powerful emotional filter
- are usually more emotionally manipulative than boys, and have advanced negotiating skills with their parents
- are likely to be ultra-sensitive to any personal comment, particularly during adolescence when their self-confidence can falter

All these factors can converge to make them outstanding managers as adults, but they can also lead to strain within the family relationships as girls grow up.

Your daughter needs to have an individual relationship with each of her parents, or parent-substitutes, whether she normally lives with these individuals or not. If you are an absent parent, use chatty emails or texts; the subtext here is that you still love her unconditionally, despite physical separation. If you live at home with your daughter, you can develop a good relationship with her by ensuring you have regular time just the two of you for relaxed conversation – for example, while doing the washing-up after supper one to one.

A girl generally needs to talk – a lot! Just chatting in an engaged way on a regular basis, from the time speech begins, will get her into the habit of talking things over. This will allow you not only to help with simple things, such as homework – but more importantly, to help steer her emotional growth, as well as to keep things going even when there are difficult times, especially at adolescence. It will enable trust to be built up between you during childhood, and for this to continue after puberty, when family relationships can become strained.

During adolescence, a girl is more likely to take up the values of her peer group than those of her family. Even if it can seem more like simply polite conversation at times, fraught with sensitive areas which must be skirted around, just keep on chatting. This way your daughter will know that, although she seems to be pushing you away, you are still there for her, and that the crucial unconditional love remains as she searches for her own personality and identity. She may often feel very lonely and lost during this stage, and it's important that she knows she has not lost the secure love of which she was certain in childhood. Remember that in order for her to become an independent, mature adult, she first needs to separate from you.

If things get very bad, or you are worried that she is not in good emotional health, talk it over with your GP or another suitable professional. If your teenage daughter is caught up with others who are not well grounded, or whose family relationships are poor, she may need qualified emotional support – or perhaps a loved and respected grandparent, aunt or godmother can help. She may turn to a teacher or family friend for adult support; if she does, you should not feel you have failed – it is normal.

Our children teach us patience. Our daughters are usually immensely companionable at almost all ages, and while they can be emotionally demanding, they repay it a thousand-fold over time. As adults, should they have children, they will treat their own children as they were treated – generously with love, but with the courage to apply appropriate boundaries at each age, and the ability to defend them as necessary. We model the people our children become. By showing them that we like to spend time with them on a daily basis, we also demonstrate that they are worth everything to us.

3

Mums and daughters — highs and lows

It starts simply enough — that dear little baby who has stolen your heart. But as she grows up, it all gets more complicated, and your heart melts a bit less when she steals your shoes and your make-up, all the mugs are in her room and she and the car are AWOL.

Maybe she is like you, and maybe not. There is often a unique closeness, as if each seems to see the other as no other can, and they both know it. Over time, the relationship can be quite a rollercoaster, but as well as being the most demanding, it can also be the most rewarding there is. For many women, it is certainly the most important relationship in their lifetime.

The fluency of speech normally developed by girls at a very young age makes possible an exceptional exchange of ideas with their mothers. However, that will include the voicing of negative thoughts as well as deeply affectionate ones. The negotiating power of a 4-year-old girl, especially with her mother, can be astonishingly complex, effective and even manipulative. It can elicit similarly complex responses from the mum, which may not be entirely adult, especially when either or both is tired, as will commonly be the case. More sleep on both sides often cures most problems!

A girl's mother is her model for life. If you want your daughter to be the best person she can be, you must model the values you wish for her. It helps you to be honest, kind, fair and rational, too, and it gives you the confidence to set appropriate boundaries within which your daughter can operate. After setting these boundaries, you must allow her to negotiate increased freedom over time, and look for reasonably safe ways by which she can become suitably independent, and make her own rules from sensible self-discipline and her own personal wisdom. It helps if you remember this relationship is there for the long term, and that, in time, it will become one of two adults, and later it may well be you who is dependent on her.

During your daughter's childhood and youth, you should not abdicate responsibility to her just because she is demanding it before she is ready – the grown-ups are supposed to be in control. However, the recognition that even a young girl can make many choices for herself without harm, and that mum should not try to control her daughter, will help both sides to enjoy their lives together as well as separately. A shared sense of humour and confident certainty that all will be well, even though work is required on both sides, will address many eventualities.

It can also help if there is a granny or granny-substitute for you and your daughter to learn from, regarding generational differences and the enduring value of good manners, hard work and respect for others. In time, as the generations move forward, you yourself are likely to be the granny; then, your daughter will suddenly appreciate you all the more. You will have the time to better understand your relationship with your daughter, as she becomes the mum with your granddaughter, and then perhaps sees her own daughter become mum, in her turn.

The changing relationship between mums and daughters

The relationship between mother and daughter is often close until secondary school, when things start to change, and not always in a comfortable way. A larger school, longer journey with more independence, plus the start of puberty, will combine to bring about changes everywhere. You may feel a loss of control for the first time – you will know so much less of your daughter's school life. The happy child who felt at the top of her tree in Year 6 is suddenly at the bottom of a much larger and more daunting edifice. She will get very tired, very fast. Typically, by the end of that first long term, she will be holding it together at school, but not so successfully at home, and everyone will know it!

You will need to get to know the person named by the school as your daughter's pastoral carer, and share any worries with them and take their experienced advice. You should try to prepare yourself for a change in your relationship, sensitively offering help at the right time and in the right way, while showing total confidence that your daughter is managing it all very well herself.

Crucially, you must keep speaking with your daughter. This will lay down a structure of support during what is often an even more difficult time ahead. A daily family evening meal keeps things smooth, and can provide an opportunity for regular one to one chats as well. If it's a school night, it helps if you can ensure that your daughter has a well-organised day. It is a parental responsibility to ensure a pupil gets to school in good time without rushing, is well prepared with all of her schoolwork ready and has eaten breakfast. It is also a parental responsibility to ensure there is a protected time and place for homework, and that she gets to bed early enough to have plenty of sleep, without watching television or using networking sites late at night.

Keeping firm boundaries, while allowing the chance for negotiation of more liberty when appropriate, will keep your daughter secure and confident. Adults must remain in control and model what they want their daughter to do – tell the truth, be open and affectionate, apologise when necessary and keep lines of communication open.

With adolescence comes a pulling away from family, which may carry a great hidden sense of loss of security, and a strong new association with a peer group. This is not a failure of family relationships, but a normal stage of progress. Ideally, an adult is there when your daughter comes home each day, and family values are re-encountered after the heady emotional dramas of school, with family chats over an evening meal. Even during the worst of times of adolescence, a mother is hugely important as a role model and steady rock. It will not always feel like that, but provided there is not a total sense of humour failure, the relationship will, unsteadily, change to one of mutual admiration and support between adults – a source of great contentment on both sides.

Dads – helping your daughter to be the best she can be

Being the dad of a daughter is a great privilege for any man, and it should be a joy. How you treat her and advise her will help to shape her opinion of herself and will affect her relationships with other men during the course of her life. Over the years, fathers invest a great deal in their daughters, but they can sometimes forget that the most important investment of all is time!

Your daughter's happiness and success, in whatever field, are not mutually exclusive, but they are interdependent. Fathers can contribute greatly to ensuring that home is a secure, nurturing environment where their daughters can make mistakes and even fail occasionally, safe in the knowledge that they will continue to be supported and loved. Therefore, it is important that you make time to support your daughter and do all you can to encourage her to try new activities and seize new opportunities. Give her the confidence to have a go, be it to audition for a part in the school play or to strive for that coveted place on the netball team. Remember, however: it is also important not to impose your own hobbies and interests on your daughter; encourage her to invest time in the activities she is interested in so that she feels ownership of them. If you can discover an interest you both share, it will provide opportunities to deepen your relationship with your daughter; otherwise, get her to teach you about her own interests – you may discover a new interest and will have learnt something from her.

Of course, there will be times when your daughter fails to

make the team or is not top of her class; however, this is about your daughter, not you! Avoid direct comparisons with your own ability or school career. Regardless of how well meaning you are, imposing your own academic expectations and choices on to your daughter, or comparing her with a sibling, cousin or colleague's child, is unlikely to be helpful and can even be hurtful. Instead, support her in setting her own achievable standards and goals.

Praise is inevitably more effective than criticism, especially with girls. Never miss an opportunity to nurture your daughter's self-esteem; after a setback, provide the loving support that will enable her to pick herself up and rise to meet her next challenge. We sometimes forget that the timing of those important or sensitive conversations can be crucial if there is to be a positive outcome. Just because you happen to be free from life's pressures momentarily, it might not be the right time for your daughter, so judge this carefully. Take the lead from her; if she wants to discuss something vital to her at 11 pm, try to prop your eyelids open and listen. Do not expect your daughter to tell you every-thing – there is a subtle difference between dad 'showing an interest' and interfering.

Time with your daughter is time well spent, but never forget how important your daughter's friends also are to her. Take the time to know them well; they are vital to your daughter's happi-ness, just like her dad. Celebrate your daughter's every success with her; after all, you have given her the confidence to throw her hat in the ring and to be the best she can be!

Dads and daughters —
your questions answered

Q: My daughter hasn't achieved the grades she should. As her dad, what can I do to help?

A: It is so important that your daughter does not feel that her lack of success is a disappointment to you and that you do not think any less of her. It might be that she has reached her potential and you are overestimating her ability, or perhaps your daughter is a little too ambitious. Talk to her teachers; they will tell you whether your daughter is working effectively and achieving her full potential or whether there is still more to come. Either way, it is great that you are there to support her as she picks herself up. Make it as easy as possible for her to have another go, but do keep an eye on reality; it may be that your daughter has done exceedingly well and should be congratulated for doing so!

Q: As a family, we have always been open and have brought up our children to not be ashamed of their bodies. Now my teenage daughter wants to lock her bedroom door and locks herself in the bathroom for hours. What's going on?

A: It is perfectly natural for your daughter to become modest, even secretive, while her body is developing. It will take her time to get used to the changes that are happening, and she is not, and may never be, ready to return to the easy confidence of childhood. She may be particularly shy around you, a male, and it is important that you do not tease or mock her natural modesty; after all, it is something you want her to develop. She may also feel that her bedroom should now become her private space into which she can invite people, including her family, rather than it being 'invaded'. Respect her wishes unless you have very good reasons to suspect negative motives for wanting this privacy.

Q: My daughter, aged 8, seems to love play-flirting with every man she comes into contact with. Should I be worried?

A: Hopefully not — practising her feminine wiles is one element of growing up. However, you will not wish your daughter only to relate to the opposite sex in a 'flirty' way. It is vital that your daughter is encouraged, particularly by her father, to value herself for who she is: her interests, talents and personality, rather than for her physical attributes. If she can learn this from an early age, she will respect herself and make wise choices later. If you are seriously concerned about her behaviour — for instance, if she shows inappropriate knowledge of sexual matters — you should consider talking to your GP about your concerns.

Q: My daughter has always had a good relationship with her mother, but now they are constantly rowing. She and I are getting along really well, but I'm uncomfortable about this friction between the two women in my life.

A: Your final phrase explains it all! Your daughter (probably aged around 14?) is challenging her mother for the 'alpha female' role in your household, questioning and testing her in her own quest to work out what sort of woman she herself is going to be. In the process she will also be vying for your attention and testing her female charms en route to womanhood. Not an easy time — but very normal! For each of you, the key to getting through this phase unscathed is for you and your partner to maintain a united front and appropriate boundaries — particularly regarding acceptable behaviour from your hormonal daughter. This is even more important if you are living apart. In this case, you could be tempted to believe everything your (currently) adoring daughter is telling you about her mother's perceived imperfections. Try to remember that this is just another developmental phase.

Family Issues

Every parent wishes for and strives to give their child a happy, nurturing and secure framework in which she can grow and thrive but inevitably your daughter will encounter setbacks and difficulties on her path to adulthood. Failure and loss are part of life and she will need your support as she comes to terms with and learns to assimilate whatever difficulties come her way. Within the family she may have to cope with bereavement or divorce, sibling rivalry or any of the other stresses and strains which are a normal part of life. It is important to separate your emotions from hers and to understand her perspective; to remember than you are the adult, she is the child. Your daughter's friends may come and go but her family should give her unconditional love and support.

Divorce and separation

The personal relationship between you as a couple may be over. You may be contemplating or have embarked upon separating or divorcing, and yet your role as parents continues.

At this difficult time never forget that your daughter still needs you. The strain of a failing emotional relationship can impact upon yours with your daughter. It is vital that you both continue to communicate clearly with her.

The key messages for parents at this time are:
- neither of you should undermine the other in front of your daughter
- both of you should avoid blaming her for the breakdown of the relationship
- both of you should set up consistent messages about boundaries with each other prior to separation
- both of you should reassure her that while your relationship has failed, your love for her is constant and continuing

Some parents seek the support of a family mediator to facilitate their communication with each other and with their children. A family mediator usually has legal or therapeutic training. They are completely independent, as they do not advise either parent individually. They do not judge the issues or impose solutions. Instead, they are able to work with both parents face to face to help see issues from the viewpoints of each child and to focus on the future rather than dwelling on the past. Mediation can help to manage the practical arrangements associated with children keeping in contact with the parent they no longer live with. While mediation is a confidential and private process, just think what a powerful message you send to your daughter by demonstrating that to sort out difficult issues, the best way is to sit down and talk about them rather than to fight.

If your daughter is having significant problems handling your relationship breakdown, consider finding someone for her to talk to, perhaps a friend of the family or a counsellor. Do keep her school informed of the situation so that her teachers can support her. They will have experience of the potential impact on your daughter and will be able to provide a safe environment for her.

Bereavement

Death is an unavoidable part of life. With death comes loss and grief, anger and disbelief.

Most of us think of bereavement as occurring primarily on the death of a loved one, but there are other kinds of bereavement. These can include difficult situations, such as when parents separate or divorce, when chronic illness becomes a reality in the home, when physical, sexual or emotional abuse is happening to a child, or even when a good friend moves away.

Feelings of bereavement can also happen when seemingly wonderful circumstances cause big changes to children's lives, such as adoption into a family, the birth of a new sibling, or the arrival of a step-parent.

Be aware that every child will respond to situations of change and loss quite differently. Your daughter may appear to adjust on her own to a significant bereavement such as the loss of a grandparent, or she may be devastated by a seemingly minor loss like the death of a pet.

Although children see loss, death and disaster on television, in films, on the internet and in books and magazines, we tend not to talk to them about the fact of death. Our generation doesn't 'do' death.

The guidance below should help in dealing with bereavement with your daughter. There are some further suggestions for sources of support at the back of this book.

- Never assume that your daughter will react to loss in the same way as you. Don't think that if she isn't crying, she isn't sad. We each have a different way of handling bereavement, and this should be respected. This is particularly important if you are also grieving.

- Don't feel as though you always need to say something deeply meaningful to her; it's enough just to be there, simply to listen or to hug her. Laugh with her; give her a chance to rant and rage; sit quietly next to her; let her cry without embarrassment or even cry with her. Ask her what she needs. She will appreciate being asked, even if her response is, 'I don't know yet.' Accept that, and let her know that you'll still be there when she does.

- Don't forget to look after yourself while you are looking after your daughter in bereavement, because every carer needs a carer.

- Try to resist saying, 'I know what you are going through; I understand what you are feeling.' Although you are trying to sympathise, your daughter is likely to say, 'No, you don't understand how I'm feeling. *I* don't even understand how I am feeling. And you don't know what I'm going through.'

And if you get it wrong and say or do something which upsets your daughter, apologise, say sorry and begin again.

A word about pets:
Don't forget that your daughter's first brush with deep grief may be the death of a pet. Don't tell her she can get another kitten, however logical that may seem. Be aware that her bereavement is very similar to the bereavement encountered at the passing of a beloved person.

A word on grieving children attending funerals:
Every family must decide whether to allow a grieving child to attend a funeral. A child may feel real anger if she is prevented from attending a significant funeral 'for her own good'. Children appreciate ritual; they need a chance to express grief publicly, as well as an opportunity to say goodbye to a loved one. Sit down with your child, tell her what happens at a funeral and what she might see and hear at one. Do try, if at all possible, to include your child in the decision-making process of whether or not she should attend.

It is very important to inform your daughter's school if she suffers any significant loss. Staff will be experienced in supporting grieving children and can offer both of you support and advice. How and what you would like the school to reveal to your daughter's classmates needs to be carefully considered and will depend on her age.

There is a wealth of material about loss, grief and bereavement in children and young people, including *Good Grief: Exploring Feelings, Loss and Death with Under Elevens* by Barbara Ward and associates. Other resources on bereavement care can be had by contacting your NHS Trust and specialist groups like Winston's Wish. Additional useful leaflets and educational documents on childhood bereavement are also available from many local children's hospices and county bereavement networks.

Bereavement and the role of schools

Every time we hear about the untimely death of a parent or child – for example, the victim of a fatal car accident, a heart attack or the fight lost to a terminal illness – our thoughts are very much with the surviving parent and the children who have lost a mother or father.

We try to imagine the enormity of the loss, of the disappearance of the source of love, of the need to come to terms with the fact that life will never be the same. Some people have a strong extended family; others have a close network of friends who provide emotional and practical support. But in spite of this, understanding and dealing with loss can be a lonely and bewildering business, even for the best-supported individual.

According to Winston's Wish (a remarkable charity which exists to support children who have lost a parent or a sibling), every 22 minutes a child in Britain is bereaved of a parent. This equates to 24,000 new children each year learning to live with a powerful range of confusing and conflicting emotions. Bottled up, these emotions can have damaging consequences in later life for the individual, their family and society as a whole.

Schools have an important role to play in supporting children who have been bereaved. The familiar routine of school is in itself a consolation to the bereaved child whose life has ceased to be normal. At the same time, teachers and other staff in caring roles, together with friends, need to accept that bereaved children, especially adolescents, will have mood swings and periods during which they challenge the importance of studying, rules and making much of an effort to look neat. This loss of drive and purpose is completely understandable and may also be accompanied by a sense of anger at the sibling or parent who has gone and resentment that they are now 'different' from their peers. The challenge for staff is to judge how much and for how long to tolerate sullen or uncooperative behaviour. Great patience and empathy are required when a child has retreated into herself, and these barriers are hard to penetrate. Time, of course, is a healer, but ensuring that a child has grieved with the support of bereavement counselling is incredibly important. Good communication between staff is vital so that, for example, Religious Studies and English teachers are mindful of the sensitivities associated with studying certain topics or texts while being aware that these may provide a helpful vehicle for expressing emotions. On a more practical level, schools are adept at providing additional coaching, from assisting with catch-up work to writing to the examination boards to seek special consideration for their candidate.

Schools also need to support the friends of someone who has experienced bereavement, and on rare but tragic occasions to cope with the death of a current pupil. Friends can be the mainstay of someone's emergence from grief, their loyalty being a source of hope, but these friends need the discreet support of the pastoral staff in handling their friend and her mood swings. Friends can sometimes be the ones to alert staff to worrying behaviour – for example, bleak thoughts posted on Facebook – but they must also not feel guilty if they need to detach themselves from the bereaved friend and get on with their own lives. They may be more use to her in this way.

When the whole school is involved in a tragedy, staff and pupils will invariably be magnificent in thinking and acting with moving sensitivity, reaching out to the extended family, as well as being resourceful. Depending on the situation, the support needs to extend through the months ahead, and it can be some time before life is back to anything resembling normal. Although no one would ever wish for such tragedies, they can bind together a community, reaffirm our humanity and remind everyone of a school's role in giving hope, even in the face of grief and adversity.

Sibling rivalry

Children frequently learn about emotions through their relationships with their siblings. Issues of conflict, friendship, social skills and, above all, how to form relationships with others are developed in childhood and can have far-reaching consequences for your daughter throughout her childhood, teenage years and indeed whole life. Sibling rivalry can last into adulthood and can be acted out over and over again in future relationships. Therefore, as parents it is important to consider your actions and how your behaviour impacts upon your daughter and your other children. This is why it is essential for parents to demonstrate consistency within the rules and structure of a family and to avoid favouring any one child.

Noel Janis-Norton, cited in Cassandra Jardine's *How to be a Better Parent*, believes that sibling rivalry is natural, and indeed even beneficial, in ensuring that children learn to share, take turns, learn tolerance and know how to handle disagreements. She advises parents not to intervene in sibling squabbles, but to tell children to take their arguments elsewhere and sort out the problem themselves, alongside the basic rule that no throwing is allowed so that nothing can be turned into a weapon of any kind! This may sound like radical advice, but children do need to learn the skills to sort out their own problems and need to learn how to resolve an argument amicably. If an argument becomes too great and there is violence and real aggression, then try doing as schools do – get the children together, with you as a facilitator, and spend some time talking through the disagreement, listening to your children and helping them to listen to each other, resolve the argument and apologise to one another.

As a parent, it is important to make time for each individual child and to give her quality time with you, ideally doing something you both enjoy. If you treat your children as individuals in their own right, they will have less need to compete for your attention with their siblings.

A new sibling

The first child is always the trailblazer, but she is also the one with whom parents first learn how to be parents. New parents are often anxious with their first child and perhaps also a touch overindulgent. It is important to teach your first child to be self-reliant, to learn how to play by herself and how to enjoy her own company. When you know you are going to have a new sibling for your firstborn, ensure that you prepare her for this. Then, once her sibling is born, give your older child even more attention so that she does not feel marginalised.

All siblings need to be treated as individuals and have their different temperaments recognised and appreciated. Older siblings will often take on the role of the teacher/helper. An older sister can often be bossier than her siblings and enjoys telling her younger brothers and/or sisters what to do. She may continue this role into later life.

The second child is less likely to get as much attention as the first and has to adapt more readily to her role as the additional child within the family. This tends to mean that the second child can be more amenable and tolerant than the older sibling. She has to fit in with the already established routines of the family and she also learns very early on that there is another child with needs and requirements.

The rules around consistency are key here. It is imperative that you ensure your daughter knows which behaviour is acceptable and which behaviour is not and that you are firm and clear about this. For example, if your toddler bites her new sibling, you may choose to punish her by giving her a 'time out' on the naughty step. However, older toddlers may like to be helpful and can be keen to assist by bringing you things to help you with the baby. Do ensure that you make time for both your children – for example, while feeding the new baby, you could read a story to your toddler. There are many books on this subject (e.g. *New Toddler Taming,* by Christopher Green) and your health visitor can also offer useful advice.

Try to continue to give quality time to each of your children. It is hard work, and some quality time for the adults doesn't go amiss either.

Older children

As your children grow older and reach school age, family patterns can become even more entrenched. The squabbles and fights between children will continue and can be over all sorts of things: television watching, toy ownership or whose turn it is to use the computer. As the parent, you must ensure that the rules are clear to the children – rules about bedtime, television watching and computer access – and you must ensure that your sanctions are consistent. Work with your partner so that the children know not to play you off against one another. Children will cleverly look for any chinks in their parents' armour – unite with your partner so that the children know that the adults remain in charge.

Younger children often mimic older ones. So, for example, in a family with more than two children, where there are teenagers beginning to push the boundaries, with different rules because of their ages, a younger sibling may begin to feel that she, too, should be allowed to do the same. As a parent, you need to make it clear that the older children have privileges because of their ages, and that she has different rules.

Your children are all different from one another and you need to celebrate those differences while maintaining harmony within the family. Simple in theory, but in practice, there will be arguments, fights and jealousies and these are part of normal family life. Consistency at all times and quality time for each individual child are essential.

Consistency and communication

As in any relationship – parent to child or parent to parent – of key concern is communication. Parents need always to maintain communication with their children as well as with one another. Parents need to try to remain impartial when there is sibling conflict, while retaining sensitivity to the needs of each individual child. They also need to be aware that the dynamic within the nuclear family affects each relationship within it as well as all the relationships that will stem from it in the future.

Struggling?

There are numerous ways in which you can gain extra help or support with your children. Your first port of call is likely to be your partner, parents or close friends. Do talk to them and ask for advice. Also, read widely, talk to your friends with children of a similar age and scour websites, such as www.MyDaughter. co.uk or www.Mumsnet.com. Perhaps attend a parenting class if you are finding parenting difficult. Finally, if you find that sibling rivalry within your family is having a detrimental impact on you all, ask your GP to refer you to a family therapist for some help and support.

Although relationships between siblings can be complex, they can also be incredibly rewarding and supportive. Siblings can form a close bond and develop friendships that last a lifetime. Hopefully your children will be able to form positive and happy relationships with their siblings, in turn enabling them to develop secure, warm and fulfilling relationships with others in the future.

The role of grandparents

The role of grandparents in your daughter's life cannot be underestimated. A grandparent – and often the grandmother, in the case of a daughter – can be a crucial support for both daughters and mothers, as she straddles both generations and can be a useful provider of both wisdom and experience.

At various stages in your daughter's life, grandparents can take on a significant role. Today, it is relatively common for grandparents to be involved in their grandchildren's lives from an early age, as grandparents are asked by their daughters to take on childcare responsibilities, instead of resorting to a nanny or daycare. Although this can be exhausting for the grandparents, it can also bring huge rewards. This set-up also provides a continuity of childcare throughout the generations as well as the passing on of a similar value system and moral code. A close relationship is forged between the child and the grandparent during the child's formative years, and this bond lasts a lifetime.

As your daughter grows up, grandparents can offer advice and support to you as a parent on the challenges of parenting, especially during the teenage years. It is also helpful as a parent to be reminded of your own teenage behaviour once upon a time! Girls can call on their grandmothers for advice about any number of things – from asking questions about various homework assignments, to calling up to chat about issues that they do not necessarily want to discuss with their own parent. A grandparent can offer a more objective voice at times and will often back up the parent in a subtle and supportive way.

In an ideal world, it is recommended that you try to ensure your daughter spends regular and quality time with her grandparents. The grandparent–grandchild relationship is an especially precious one and it should be nurtured and developed into a mutually rewarding experience for all parties concerned.

Tricky situations

Separation

In the case of a recent separation or divorce between two parents, your daughter is often suffering greatly and she cannot always understand the problems of an adult world. At this time, grandparents can step in and offer valuable additional support, as well as the provision of another place where your daughter can feel safe and secure. Encourage your daughter to turn to her grandparents when necessary; allow her to simply be a grandchild, to feel loved and occasionally spoilt; and let her know there is somewhere else where she can go and process her emotions. If you are going through a marital break-up as a parent, do allow your own parents to support you and your children. Their support for the whole family cannot be underestimated. Swallow your pride and allow them to take on this role for all of you. Your parents love you, just as you love your own children, and they will do their utmost to help you through the most difficult of situations.

Difficult grandparents

The world is made up of very different people with different expectations and value systems. Sometimes, your child's grandparents do not share your views on life and parenting techniques. This can occasionally be the case with the 'in-laws', but it is important to try to forge a relationship with your child's grandparents, even if they are difficult. Establish ground rules as early as you can and try to stick to them. For example, try to set up a monthly visit to allow them to see their grandchildren. You can decide where and when you should meet. Try to agree on a set of rules regarding your parenting rules and theirs.

If there are difficulties with your in-laws, do discuss this with your partner as sensitively as you can so that you both work together for the benefit of your children. However, if you find that the visits are unbearable, try to seek some professional help

– for example, from a family therapist – to see whether you can facilitate some regular contact for the sake of your children. As your children grow older, you don't want them to criticise you as a parent for depriving them of their grandparents; equally, as your children grow into their teenage years and beyond, they will begin to be able to make their own decisions about whether they want to have a relationship with their grandparents.

Geography

Gone are the days when extended families lived close together, and distance can make the relationship between grandparents and grandchildren very complicated. If your daughter's grandparents live far away, encourage them to maintain regular contact by telephone, email or even Skype or Facebook! Your daughter can teach her grandparents to work out the new technologies – just as a 10-year-old girl can teach her 70-year-old grandmother to text!

As with all long-distance relationships, when your child's grandparents live far away, the time spent together is often intense due to the infrequency of the visits. Do make allowances for the visiting grandparents and try to make the visits as enjoyable as possible. Research local activities in your area, find out what is on at the cinema and save up some enjoyable outings to do together whenever a visit comes up. In this way, both parties can look forward to the visit with excitement.

As your daughter grows up, try to develop a relationship in which she can spend quality time with her grandparents, such as a weekend away. In addition to a lovely time between granddaughter and grandparents, this also provides the additional perk of some much needed respite for the parents!

Working grandparents

Many grandparents still work full time, which means that their time is limited and they may not be able to take on the additional responsibilities of looking after grandchildren. It is important to respect working grandparents and not to assume that they are available at your beck and call. They have done their childrearing and they are not obliged to do it a second time around! Most working grandparents will be amenable to being the 'back-up' and will welcome quality time with their grandchildren, but on their own terms. Remember, what is crucial in all relationships is the need to communicate clearly and to be respectful of one another.

Family Life and Homework

Maintaining happy families – how to avoid the homework fights
From her very first reading book to her A level essays, your daughter will have work to do at home. But how best to help her without it becoming the all too familiar burden that can blight the whole family's evenings and weekends? Bearing in mind that perhaps your daughter may have a long journey to school, she needs to eat and have time for other interests and the opportunity to 'flop' – and there are family commitments that need to be fitted in. How can you make homework work for both her and you?

As with many situations as a parent, you need to perform a balancing act – to be supportive but not to interfere! Here are some tips to help keep you on track:

- Remember, each of us works differently. Some like to get work out of the way and then relax, others work better if they've relaxed first. If your daughter is one of the latter, no amount of nagging will get her to work efficiently before she's had a chance to relax.
- Ensure she has an appropriate place to work – and, yes, curled up on the sofa with the television on in the background may be fine for some work, as may an MP3 player.
- Ensure she has some time each evening to relax, and time during the week for other activities apart from homework.
- Show an interest and offer to help if she wants you to.

- Don't insist on checking her work and giving unasked-for advice on improving it.
- Don't do it for her. If she's really struggling, it's better to discuss with her when she can see the relevant teacher, preferably before the deadline to hand it in.

Be particularly careful with work for public examinations. Exam boards will penalise a candidate severely if they think the work is not their own.

Try to prevent homework becoming a battleground, as this might ultimately harm the relationship between you and your daughter. If you find that your daughter really isn't coping with homework, then talk to the school. As much as you, they want her to be able to achieve her best, and homework is an integral part of that.

Thoughts from a Head — stop bashing parents . . .

Being a parent has to be the hardest job in the world. A Head Teacher was struck by a comment from a parent who pointed out that when you are at work, you have regular feedback about the job you're doing — a review with a line manager, a pat on the back for a task well done, even a bonus in the good old days. But a parent gets very little in terms of positive reinforcement, and listening to the news can suggest that all of society's ills can be laid at the parents' door.

While it can be the hardest job in the world, it can also be one of the most joyful and rewarding. Parenting can certainly be made easier if schools and parents work together in the best interests of the children, and this is something at which many schools are adept.

It is the dual responsibility of parents and schools to ensure that children are properly prepared for life, encouraged to achieve their best inside the classroom and outside it and taught to develop a healthy sense of social responsibility. This will involve instilling in young people a conviction that they should do the right thing because it is the right thing, rather than in hope of reward or out of fear of punishment. We want our children to aim for a life well lived, involving sensitivity to and care for others (rather than a pure focus on self), speaking out against bullying in all its forms and showing disapproval of blatant injustice or prejudice.

There are many ways in which schools and parents can work in concert to ensure that the children at the heart of this relationship receive the support and guidance they need to be their best, during their years at school and in their lives beyond. Good schools and responsible parents provide young people with a secure framework within which to make their own choices and decisions, as well as their own mistakes. We know we cannot live children's lives for them. We cannot prevent them from occasionally getting it wrong, and it can be disheartening for parents to see their children making the same mistakes that they themselves made. But these are their mistakes to make, painful though that might be, and a loving parent has to help their offspring deal with the disappointment of such experiences and move forward. Parents cannot be held responsible for the unwise choices their children may sometimes make.

A school governor suggested that, in a sense, we erect scaffolding around our children, but, as they grow older, we need to begin to dismantle it. By the time they are 18 and about to leave home for university or join the world of work, they should be standing tall and secure without the degree of structured support they may have needed when they were younger. They may find that they are now living independently and caring for themselves without parents on hand and without the monitoring and guidance they will have received at school. They will need to be sufficiently organised, motivated and self-disciplined so that they can pace their work and get the balance right. Some may be tempted to work too hard; more will be tempted not to work hard enough. By this stage, schools and parents together should have equipped them with the skills they will need not only to survive, but also to flourish in their new state of independence.

So how can we work together to provide the framework and to give the girls and boys in our schools the tools they need to do the job? Firstly, we need recognition that education, in its widest sense, is the job of all of us. It is naive and misleading to suggest that schools educate academically and parents instil moral values. It is impossible to see education in a narrow sense as somehow divorced from moral values. Schools and parents need to work together to ensure these young people live well, achieving their best within the classroom and outside it and developing a healthy sense of social responsibility.

Secondly, parents need to ensure that their children are able to take responsibility, including for those things they get wrong. If your son or daughter is in trouble at school, leaping to their defence isn't necessarily in their best interests, however comforting it might feel. If a child has made an unwise choice, working with the school to give clear messages and to ensure that your son or daughter knows where the parameters are (and which boundaries they have crossed) will help them far more than being 'in their corner'. With a truculent teenager at home, it seems like too good an opportunity to miss being on their side against the perceived common enemy at school. A Deputy Head reported an incident of dealing with a girl who was suspected of being responsible for writing graffiti in a school toilet. The father waded in, outraged that his daughter would ever be accused of doing such a thing. It took the wind out of his sails somewhat when the Deputy Head told him that she had openly admitted she had done it before he arrived.

Returning to the comment of the parent who yearned for positive feedback on her parenting, this is something that Heads quite frequently offer. When we sit down together to discuss a particular issue, especially if the parent is trying to set boundaries and meeting resistance, Heads will quite often say, 'You are doing the right things.' It is important to tell parents not to apologise for caring about and worrying about their children, even when this occasionally makes them overly passionate. Parents are encouraged to be strong, to appreciate that, despite the resistance, children do want and need boundaries, as boundaries reassure them that they are loved. And, of great importance — Heads try very hard not to bash the parents. We are all on the same side — which is, of course, the children's.

Family Q&A

Fraught families – keep talking . . .

Q: My 12-year-old daughter had a terrible row with my mother-in-law (her grandmother) a month ago and said some terrible things, calling her names, etc. She is going through a bad time: her father and I have recently separated and she had some friendship issues at school. Her grandmother now doesn't want anything to do with her and has written a letter criticising my parenting. What should I do — just let the dust settle or write back?

A: It's important to keep communicating, even when relationships are not going smoothly. Try writing to your mother-in-law, apologising on behalf of your daughter and explaining how difficult she is finding your recent separation. Then you could say how sorry you are that she doesn't want to see her granddaughter at the moment. Emphasise the importance of a grandparent's role, particularly when parents are separating, and remind her of how awkward teenagers can be, even at the best of times. Finally, state that, of course, you will respect her wishes but will welcome her back when she feels the time is right, wishing her well in the meantime.

Q: My partner and I are going through a difficult patch but are trying to protect our daughter from any effects of our dispute. Is this possible?

A: Parents' individual problems can influence the dynamic within a family, and a child can often 'act out' when the conflict gets too much. So, for example, it is often the case that younger siblings will mimic parents' arguments, using the same language and tone of voice, and often will be physically aggressive with one another to express their frustrations. Your older daughter may start to develop faddy eating habits or perhaps begin to self-harm. All these are examples of ways in which children will aim to divert attention away from the arguing parents and instead become the focus of the attention themselves. Teenagers will often do this subconsciously as a way of ensuring that their parents will have to come together, even if only to talk about the troubled teenager.

Do not underestimate the effect of what you do as parents and how this can impact upon your daughter and your other children. Children are very sensitive to arguments, and they pick up on conflict in relationships and may act this out within their play or with their friends. For example, if your daughter starts having complex friendship issues with her school friends, perhaps think of what could be happening at home that is upsetting and unsettling her.

Above all, keep the lines of communication open both with your children and with each other, and don't be afraid to turn to external sources for help. There are some listed in the back of this book.

Q: How do I keep the channels of communication open without my daughter thinking I am neurotic?

A: It is important that your daughter knows how to communicate with you and for you to know the best ways in which to communicate with her. Talk to your daughter about what she would prefer — whether you should check in with her in person, by phone or by text. Try to do it in an unobtrusive way, but remind her that you are checking up on her as you are concerned about her personal wellbeing and safety. It may also be useful to have the mobile phone numbers of some of her friends so you can drop them a brief text if you are unable to get hold of your daughter. However, be careful only to use these numbers in an emergency.

Q: *Why is my daughter always so horrible to me, yet can wrap her father around her little finger?*

A: The relationship between mothers and daughters is probably both the most fruitful and the most fraught there is. The daughter often overidentifies with the mother and feelings of hate and love are frequently intertwined. The mother is fully aware of the perils and pitfalls that may occur during her daughter's teenage years and she feels deeply protective of her. A father, on the other hand, sees his beautiful daughter emerging and is charmed by her. Both parents (whether living together or apart) should agree ground rules for their daughter (and, of course, other children) and stick to them. Giving a daughter a consistent message and setting realistic boundaries is vital and she will thank her parents for it.

Q: *How do I handle my daughter's mood swings?*

A: Show an interest in your daughter's schooling, friends and hobbies, but not to the extent of smothering her. Communication is vital; spend time listening to her and try to be flexible over some things and aim to avoid confrontation. If she continues to shout and rant and rave, try not to shout back; remember, you are the adult in the situation, even if your daughter knows how to push all your buttons. Walk away if you can and try to restart the conversation when you are both calm. Try to think of teenage tantrums in the same way as toddler tantrums, as this may make it easier.

Q: What boundaries should I set for my daughters regarding curfew/time to be home at night?

A: Teenagers need boundaries. They may not like being told to be home by a certain time, but as responsible parents you are showing that you care, and ultimately your teenager will value this and feel secure. Agree a time and then ask her to text you so that you know she is on her way home. This is less intrusive than a phone call, but can be equally reassuring. If your daughter is travelling by public transport, ensure that she is with others, even if this means a couple of additional teenagers staying over for the night. Alternatively, agree where and when you will collect her, and make sure that you are always there on time. Try to ensure that you are discreet when you pick her up. Don't cross-examine her about her evening; wait and allow her to tell you what she has been up to. If possible, it is helpful to do a rota with some of your daughter's friends' parents, as this takes the pressure away from you.

Q: How do I know if I should trust my daughter when she tells me where and who she is going out with?

A: You have to build a relationship of trust and mutual respect. You need to be aware that trust has as much to do with your relationship with your daughter as it does with her behaviour. When extending trust, you need to make it clear that when giving it, you require the truth. Your daughter needs to know for certain that you can survive the truth — even if it is occasionally ugly — and that so can she. Talking to her regularly about concerns regarding school work, friends, social situations and potential pitfalls lets your daughter know where you stand and why. All relationships in life are predicated on trust and honesty. Your daughter needs to know that actions have consequences, but if she is honest, your relationship will survive.

Q: How do I respond when my daughter tells me the 'ugly truth'?

A: If your daughter has the guts to tell you at the age of 13 that, for example, she got drunk at a party, the fact she has told you means that she has been frightened by this and is asking for your support to help her make better decisions. It may not feel like this at the time, but if you severely punish her, then why would she continue to confide in you? You need to help your daughter move on from unfortunate incidents and ensure that she knows how to be safe and secure the next time. It isn't easy; but if you keep the doors of communication open, she will confide in you. Always remember that you are instilling in your daughter a moral code for her future. If your daughter tells you that she thinks she may be pregnant, take a deep breath and remember that she has told you because she wants you to help her. Take her to the doctor and try to support her through the situation.

Friends

Girls' friendships can be lifelong and your daughter is likely to need your help and guidance as she acquires the skills necessary to form healthy friendships. She may have to deal with bullies or with over-intense relationships, with jealousy, rivalry and perhaps betrayal. As she grows up her peer group will become increasingly influential and you will want to help her maintain her personal integrity while integrating with her group. Your daughter's friendships will shape her identity, affirm her sense of worth and will also affect the sort of young woman she grows into. But they are also the source of great joy, strength and, above all, fun!

Best friends for ever

From a young age, girls start to develop friendships, and their importance grows as they get older. As with family relationships, they are usually multi-layered, very complex and heavily charged with powerful emotions.

Girls typically talk – and talk and talk. They can end up talking about each other, and this can translate to 'bitchiness'. This is all the more distressing when carried out by text or email, and your daughter needs to learn not to get involved in such things, and to only talk about others if it is kind, true and necessary (or at least two of these things).

In general, friendships are especially important for identity-development during adolescence, and group-loyalty can be extreme. Girls' friendships can be lifelong, and can be even closer than those of sisters. For the most part, these friendships develop through communication, shared experience and the development of loyalty.

Loyalty to friends can be paramount, and when a friend is disloyal, it can be the sudden and immediate end of that relationship, with no second chance. This may seem extreme to us as parents, but the point works both ways, and the needs of a friend may trump any obligations within a family, for fear of being seen as disloyal.

Typically, there comes a stage in many girls' lives when they have, or would like to have, a close best friend, to whom they appear completely joined, emotionally. Lovely though this can be, it can exclude the development of other friendships, leaving a girl exposed to immense emotional loss should the friendship founder, as it probably will at some point. You may become aware that your daughter is being harmed by a manipulative and emotionally needy friend, and it can take skilled conversations over a period of time to help your daughter retain the friendship at a less deep level. This will help her to tell the friend that she still likes her and enjoys her company, but she retains her own identity and self-authority so will not always do what her friend wants. This may strengthen the healthy side of the friendship, or it may cause it to fade.

Top tips:
- Get to know the families of your daughter's close friends. If a school has receptions or parents' meetings, it is worth seeking out the parents of your daughters' friends; you will be glad of each other's support with respect to behavioural guidelines as your daughters travel through adolescence together, but even before that, play-dates, birthday parties and shared lifts are appreciated on both sides.
- If your daughter finds it difficult to make friends for any reason, tell her teacher, and ask for ideas as to what you can do, and what the school can do, to help her in this. If it is not successful, you may find that you have to arrange social gatherings with other families so at least your daughter knows other children or young people. Some girls do find it hard to make friends and may not achieve it easily until the sixth

form, if that. For more on this, read 'My daughter doesn't have any friends', also in this section.

- Most parents encourage their daughter's friends to visit. If taken on holiday, however, you may find a week can sometimes be as much as girls' friendships can cope with.
- Encourage your daughter to have several good friendships, even if there is one special friend.
- Enjoy your daughter's friendships – for many parents, one of the great unsung joys of parenthood is getting to know their daughter's friends, right into adulthood.

When friendships go wrong

Why are friendships so important to girls – and why is it the end of the world when they go wrong?

Most girls want to have friends – someone to share secrets with, who looks out for them each morning and who'll miss them when they're absent. But, beyond that, your daughter's choice of friends says a great deal about her, both to her and to others.

Alongside how she dresses, her choice of friends is a large part of the image she wants to portray – she's popular, part of the 'in-crowd'. In short, she's worth knowing. And here's the proof: other girls like her, and the 'cooler' they are, the greater her standing in the wider social group.

Within the group, it's a safe place for her to try out ideas and opinions. It builds her confidence to know that her friends agree with her, be it about world issues or that must-have shade of nail varnish. There's also a lot of sharing of concerns. Worries about health, parents, boys, exams – all are shared, and frequently in great detail, with friends often sworn to secrecy. And because, for many girls, the need to belong is so strong, their groups tend to become exclusive and, although they may be friendly towards other girls, there are often very clear boundaries between friendship groups.

So, when it goes wrong, it *is* the end of the world for your daughter because now she's lost part of her identity, she's lost her place in the social order and her support structure for her ideas. Those shared secrets are now regretted. The former friends know everything about her. Now that the bond is broken, they might tell. Worse, they might be laughing at her. And the fact that she's been part of an exclusive group means that it's harder to join a new group, at least for a while.

So, when the worst happens, how can you help your daughter through the experience?

- Don't underestimate how important this is to her. It is the end of her world, as she knows it.
- Let her know you understand that – and how hurt she feels – and be prepared for her to show real grief over the loss.
- Ask her if she thinks there's any way back. Did she upset them in some way? Does she need to see if she can put that right? What would be the best way to do that?

If the distress is extreme or prolonged, it's worth letting someone at school know – perhaps her form tutor or Head of House or Head of Year. It may be appropriate for them to get involved but, if nothing else, they can offer support as she finds her way through.

Do resist the temptation to contact the parents of the other girls involved – unless she has asked you to and you're offering an olive branch on her behalf. One more layer of involvement usually makes it even harder for the girls to work things out themselves. And afterwards, whether or not the friendship is restored, take the opportunity to speak with your daughter and to help her to learn from the experience. Those lessons will stand her in good stead for the rest of her life.

My daughter doesn't have any friends

Seeing your daughter unhappy because she doesn't have friends is heart-rending as you watch her confidence ebb away and send her off to school each day after the enforced cheerfulness of breakfast.

How can you best support her?
* Acknowledge that not having friends at school is tough. Don't be dismissive of how she feels and, if appropriate, share your own experiences with her – most of us can think of times when we felt we didn't 'belong'.
* If she has friends outside of school, make sure she has plenty of contact with them so that she knows she has people who like and accept her.
* Talk to her about her day at school. Which times are the most difficult? Before school? Breaks? Lunchtimes?

Offer some practical suggestions:
* If being in the form room before school means everyone else is chatting in groups, where else could she go? The library? Another room? Can she make sure she's got something to do so she's keeping herself busy?
* At breaks and lunchtimes, what clubs or extracurricular activities could she go to? Art club? Spanish club? Table tennis? She may claim not to know what's on offer and you may need to contact the school to get the details but, if she can find something to do for most lunchtimes, it will help fill that lonely void between lunch and the start of afternoon school – and she might find a like-minded friend.
* Are there any opportunities for her to help other pupils? Listening to younger ones read? Helping to coach sports? Helping in the library?
* Can she get involved with a drama production? Volunteering to help backstage if not actually performing, or handing out programmes?

- Can she identify any other girls who seem to be by themselves? They could agree to meet up at break. They may not become close friends, but there's comfort in having the arrangement.
- Are there any new girls who seem to be on their own and might like someone to help them settle in?

As a parent, the real difficulty is that your daughter's confidence is likely to be very low. She may find making the kind of approaches mentioned above too difficult and may just say no to anything you suggest, not least because she's afraid of failing again.

If you've reached that stage, you probably need to speak with the school, specifically with one of the staff in charge of pastoral care. They are best placed to quietly help your daughter in school and they can unobtrusively arrange things for her to be involved in. Hopefully, her confidence will then increase and she'll be able to make friends for herself.

Friendship Q&A

No way to treat a friend

Q: My 12 year old daughter has a group of friends, and at the moment when she walks up to meet them (at break, for example), they giggle and run off. Two of these 'friends' usually get the school bus home with her but lately are getting a different bus and not telling her. I just do not know how to help. She is not a giggly, silly girl but her friends are; I don't think she joins in when they are being silly. She has told me that sometimes she finds them a bit boring but obviously wants to be part of the group. She is a bright girl and does want to do well, but sadly this is not seen as 'cool'. She says she does not understand why they run off, as 'it's no way to treat a friend'. Can you offer any advice? Children spend a lot of time at school and I hate to think of her being unhappy.

A: This situation is very common indeed. In each year group in every school, there will be girls who exert their influence by controlling who can and cannot be part of their group. This is agony for girls in Years 7, 8 and 9 and needs help and intervention. In each year group, there will be quite a large number of girls who wish to be 'cool' and belong to this type of friendship group. However, there will be others who are sensible, kind and caring and just want to get on with their work and activities. Your daughter needs to join a group of more similar-minded girls. This might be helped by joining in with some new extracurricular activities or finding different places to sit in class and at lunchtimes.

You may need to ask for the help of your daughter's Head of Year or tutor who should talk to the girls involved and explain that this behaviour is unacceptable. If you are not happy with the outcome, go to a member of the senior leadership team. If change is to happen, adult intervention will be needed. In addition, your daughter may need your help to stand up to the girls and tell them that their behaviour is unpleasant. You might suggest what she could say the next time they ignore her.

She's my best friend, but am I hers?
Q: My 14-year-old daughter likes school, but she seems generally unhappy and I think it is to do with problems she has being accepted by some of the other girls. She has a best friend and they do things together, but the friend is very popular and gets invited to lots of parties and sleep-overs by other girls while my daughter never seems to get invited. She says she hates it when they are all talking

about what they did the night before and she wasn't there and she thinks they do it deliberately to spite her. Do you think there is anything I or her teachers could do about it without showing her up in front of others?

A: Girls' friendships are crucial to their sense of themselves, their confidence and their wellbeing. When friendships are not going well, every other aspect of their lives can be affected. Some girls have the happy knack of making friends easily; others need support and guidance on how to gain, nurture and keep friends, as well as how to be a good friend. This is where you, as her mother, can offer your own experiences.

From what you say, your daughter knows how to make and grow one special friendship but has not yet appreciated that having a wider circle is healthier. This is most probably why she feels that these other girls are deliberately excluding and mocking her. It's far more likely that they are simply being thoughtless rather than that they are trying to make her unhappy.

The problem is that, just as you cannot force children to eat, you cannot force them to be friends. As her mother, what you can do to aid your unhappy daughter is to help her to develop strategies for surviving disappointment and for making a wider range of friends. It is dangerous for her to be so dependent on just one friend. As people grow up, they evolve and change, so having lots of friends is safer. After all, your daughter may not always want to be close to her current 'best friend', even if she cannot imagine such a situation right now. Has your daughter tried asking a wider group of girls to join her in an activity? Has she quietly asked her friend why she is not being invited on these sleepovers?

Ask her to try both these strategies, as well as encouraging her to develop new interests, perhaps ones that her friend doesn't have, so that she can meet a whole new set of potential friends. If she is still feeling isolated, try contacting her form teacher to ascertain whether she appears to be isolated at school. If so, her school should be able to suggest further strategies for you both. Nobody would claim that the teenage years are easy; good friendships can really help.

My daughter's best friend is too clingy

Q: My 10-year-old daughter has had a best friend for over a year now. However, she is starting to find her a bit clingy. She still likes her but she wants to spread her wings a bit and is not sure how to do this without upsetting her. Any advice?

A: The intensity of 'best friendships' can be a double-edged sword — a source of tremendous happiness, but also the cause of real anxiety when things cool off a bit, or the two friends mature at different rates, and therefore begin to want different things. Quite understandably, your daughter wants to be really kind in separating a bit, and it would certainly be kinder if the impetus for this separation isn't seen as coming from her. You can do a lot to help mastermind this, and she will benefit from your help. Start looking at times when they meet outside school and think about cutting these down. There may be all sorts of reasons that you can find to need your daughter at home more, or out with you more often. If your daughter is able to say to her friend, for example, that she is sorry she can't see her after school on Thursdays now because you want her to do something else, then you will start to break the dependence.

Talk to your daughter's school as well, as they will be able, unobtrusively, to engineer things so that your daughter and her friend are not always together, and are put in different groups and perhaps do different activities, so that they spend more and more time with others. Together, these strategies, with everyone working diplomatically in the background, will ease their separation and yet should mean that they can remain really good friends — the ideal outcome.

Why does my daughter sabotage her friendships?

Q: Since my daughter was a little girl (she is an only child), she has been in constant fights with her friends. As a result, she is now 15 and has no friends. Her pattern is to make a friend and after a few months there are always comments such as 'My friend is not very nice' or 'She did this or that.' An argument then occurs, and after she leaves this friend, or they leave her, my daughter goes on to another friend and so on. I have talked to her on many occasions about this. We have moved countries often, but I have always tried to make her feel secure. Is it because she feels insecure that she sabotages her friendships?

A: One of the hardest things about friendships is learning that other people rarely do exactly what we want them to do. When we were little, our world revolved around us, and we played with toys that stayed where we put them and acted as we wanted them to act. Real-life friends are much more interesting, but also very much more their own people. Until we realise that our friends are not just toys, or extensions of ourselves, and until we accept that there must be lots of tolerance and negotiation in any friendship, then we never really make lasting friendships. It sounds very much as though your daughter is still caught in a more immature approach to friendship — not because she feels insecure, but because she just hasn't yet learnt the value of not being able to control other people, but just accepting them for who they are. She may be a perfectionist — not at all uncommon! — and she would benefit from realising that imperfection is sometimes much better than perfection, certainly when it comes to relationships with other human beings. It is worth you speaking to her in these terms, showing her that you understand, and if you have any 'wise mentors' around to whom you think she might listen (e.g. your friends, aunts, her teachers and tutors and other parents — possibly even a counsellor), then talk to them and see if they can help you to reinforce these messages. You all want her to be happy, and friendships most definitely will be a part of this happiness, when she learns to 'live and let live'.

Friendships with boys

Q: My daughter is moving to an all-girls' school in September, but I am worried about how she will retain her friendships with boys or create new ones as she gets older. She doesn't have a brother and I don't want her to become awkward around boys as she hits adolescence. Any ideas?

A: On a practical level, both you as a parent and your daughter's school can, and should, create opportunities for natural friendships to occur. If your daughter's school has a 'friendly brother school', then these opportunities are part of the natural pattern of a school: music, drama, Combined Cadet Force, careers events, etc. all provide the natural openings for friendships to develop.

At home, you can also help by ensuring that activities are not just girl-friendly — for example, badminton or tennis clubs, drama groups and orchestras — and holidays could involve activities with others: adventure holidays, skiing, camping, etc.

If we teach our girls to be confident and self-assured, they should be able to create and maintain healthy relationships with anyone they come into contact with later in life. Of girls who attended all-girls' schools or mixed schools, with and without brothers, it is their inherent character that dictates how they will handle relationships — all we can do is give them the experiences that will teach them how to develop.

Sexual relationships

Your daughter will face unprecedented pressures as she enters her teenage years – to conform and to compete – and the advice you give her and the example you set her will be crucial. Raising girls in today's world can seem a daunting prospect. Unsuitable role models, media obsessed with sex and size . . . no wonder your daughter feels under pressure. While every parent would like to shelter their daughter from too much knowledge and experience too soon, it is just not possible to protect her forever. You will want your daughter to make informed decisions and to take care of herself. Although sex is an emotive, sensitive and potentially embarrassing subject it is important that your daughter can turn to you for information and advice.

Sex education by the wised-up parent

When Wet Wet Wet sang 'Love Is All Around', they probably meant not love but sex. Yes, it's everywhere – TV, films, magazines, adverts, music, newspapers, novels, the internet – there's hardly any escaping it, and most of it is aimed at the teenage market.

Sex is so flaunted, it can't be a surprise to anyone that many bright youngsters are keen to try it out as quickly as is reasonably possible. When Mae West said of men, 'I feel like a million, but one at a time', she was regarded as very 'outré'. In the 21st century, there's no need to snigger at the double entendre. It's all out there, from the casual acceptance of frequent one-night stands in *Friends*, to the full frontal nudity of *Sex and the City* (actually rated 15, but the film treat of choice for many 12 to 14 year olds' birthday parties on its release).

A striking feature of even the most intelligent teenagers is their inability to foresee consequences. So what can the concerned parent do to help them handle the immense pressure to want too much too young? It's not easy, without nagging or sounding like the harbinger of doom, but that old chestnut of 'keeping the lines of communication open' really is the answer:

- Watch their soaps with them and give your opinion, then listen honestly to theirs.
- Check that they really do have proper information – what did the school nurse say about contraception in Personal, Social and Health Education (PSHE)?
- What can your daughter tell you about sexually transmitted infections? (There are lots of new ones since most parents were young. Let your daughter be the expert in giving you that information.)

Tell them about some of your anonymous friends' experiences. Was X's abortion really painless and hassle-free? How did your colleague cope with the news that she had chlamydia, or worse? The papers are full of stories about 'love cheats', but how did that feel when it happened to you?

Let them know why and when you are worried. Sex was designed by nature to produce babies. Pleasing a current boyfriend is one thing; raising his child for the next 20 years is quite another. On the other hand, pelvic inflammatory disease can lead to infertility, and no babies at all, ever, can be devastating.

Don't sit down for a two-hour 'birds and bees' session, but chat about these things as they arise, laugh about them when you can and your daughter will be grateful of the chance to discuss issues that might well be worrying her too, with someone who knows a bit more and whom she doesn't have to impress. You will never stop her having sex but if she can keep you in the loop, it is much more likely to be safer and more at a time when she's ready than it might otherwise be.

What should I be telling my daughter about sex, and when?

The recent debate about sex education and what should/shouldn't be taught in schools, including the discussion about how much choice faith schools should have in what they teach, may have struck a chord with parents who are themselves debating what they should be talking to their daughters about, and when.

Sex and relationships education is recognised as one of the trickiest subjects for parents to broach. A 2009 survey commissioned by the Girls' Schools Association entitled 'How Well Do You Know your Daughter?' identified that across the sample of the 1,000 parents of girls who responded, sex education was the most difficult topic of conversation of all. Nevertheless, most of us will recognise that nothing is as dangerous as ignorance, and failing to address the subject, or leaving it too late, could be a high-risk strategy. So what should you tell your daughters, and when, and how might this dovetail with what they may be learning at school?

Firstly, ensure you know what your daughter's school is covering and at what stage. Usually, Sex and Relationships Education (SRE), as it is now often called, will be included in Personal, Social and Health Education (PSHE). This will be complemented by what pupils might learn about reproduction in Science or Biology, but it is important that young people receive more than just the biological facts. It is in the emotional repercussions of becoming aware of, and interested in, the opposite (or same) sex that is where the real need for learning and information arises. If we do not provide this in our schools and families, girls, in particular, will turn to some of the dubious teenage magazines on the market, or 'soaps', in their attempt to find the answers.

PSHE is a subject focusing on a range of issues beyond the formal curriculum that young people need to learn in order to lead healthy, balanced lives. The content of a school's PSHE programme will be suited to the pupil's age and stage of development. A well thought out and professionally delivered PSHE programme will help young people to develop their skills so that in time they can make their own informed choices. It should provide accurate information and a safe forum within which to explore values and attitudes, guarding against misinformation and intolerance. Ask your daughter's school for details so that you are aware of how SRE fits into the overall PSHE scheme.

At junior school level, perhaps from Year 3 (age 7) onwards, it may be that SRE focuses on the 'relationships' element, building on what the children know about friendships and families. They may be encouraged to reflect on and learn more about feelings and behaviour. When discussing families, they may well have the opportunity to consider the different kinds of family that we find in contemporary society, and there may be some exploration into how to cope with changes in our families, something that growing numbers of children need to learn. At age 7 onwards, children may also be taught the correct names for all parts of the human body. Later in the primary school years, girls may learn about growing and changing, about puberty and what this means, the onset of menstruation and how feelings change with the arrival of adolescence. By the end of Year 6 (age 11) and the last year of primary education, it is probable that pupils have received lessons about love and what a loving relationship is, the part that sex plays within a loving relationship and basic information about sexual intercourse, 'safe sex', birth control and birth itself.

If you have a daughter of junior school age and you know what is being discussed in SRE and at what stage, you can supplement this in your own conversations with her, find out what she feels about the things she is learning and whether she has any questions about them. It should be possible to do this naturally and relatively easily, without the sense that you are having an 'important discussion' and telling her things for the first time.

Parents can request that their daughters are withdrawn from SRE lessons if they feel uncomfortable about what is taught, how it is taught and at what age, and parents who wish to do so should contact the school to discuss it – but be careful. We may feel a natural impulse to protect our children and to worry about them growing up too quickly. However, we do have to accept that ignorance is much more harmful than knowledge, that this curriculum is all about giving children information to help them to make wise choices, and that ultimately we have to educate children rather than try to shield them. We need our daughters to have the skills and knowledge to enable them to cope with reality, rather than attempting to keep it at bay. There is no evidence that giving information early leads to early experimentation; in fact, the reverse is more likely to be true – shrouding sex and relationships in mystery can do more harm than being open and honest with our children. In addition, consider how your daughter might feel if the other children realise she is sitting out of these lessons.

As girls move through the secondary school years from age 11 onwards, these topics are likely to be revisited in an age-appropriate way so that girls are helped to understand the changes in their bodies and emotions. They need to develop healthy self-esteem and the confidence to resist negative peer pressure, or pressure they may feel from the way in which sex and relationships are portrayed in the media. They should develop the range of skills they need to make choices and decisions they feel comfortable with at the right time for them. They will learn about contraception, sexually transmitted infections, homosexuality and women's health issues. Again, talk to your children about what they are learning and how they feel about it. You may well find they are far better informed than you were at the same age.

In summary, good schools and caring parents help to construct a responsible framework within which our sons and daughters will make their own choices and decisions, and even, at times, their own mistakes. Parents know we cannot live their lives for them, but by communicating openly with them and working together with our children's schools, we can educate them wisely, and nowhere is this more important than in their education about happy and healthy relationships.

Why haven't I got a boyfriend?

Why do girls feel the pressure to have boyfriends earlier than parents might wish? The problem may be that girls often want to conform. They don't want to stand out, which can lead to them wanting to wear the same clothes, follow the same music and share the same enthusiasms as their peers. Having a boyfriend can seem like a badge of honour – something those they admire and look up to have – and they want to be included in this particular club. They want to prove that they're 'normal' – that they are as popular and attractive as other girls. It's also a trend, like following a fashion. It gives them something to talk to other girls about. It adds drama to their lives and it imitates adult behaviour.

Girls are very much interested in relationships of all kinds – they care far more about friendships than boys generally do (which is why fluctuations in friendship patterns can cause girls such pain). Moving into the world of boyfriends (and attracting the envy of those who are still outside this 'magic circle') is important to them. But as is the case in later life, being with the wrong partner is not preferable to being alone. Girls need to be helped to see that you start going out with someone because you are strongly attracted to each other (and it has to be mutual) and you want to spend time together. It isn't a question of first wanting a boyfriend and second seeing who is available who might fill the vacancy.

Girls have to be able to feel sufficiently good about themselves, to value themselves enough, to wait until the time is right. They need to be supported to resist the pressure to measure their popularity according to whether or not they have a boyfriend. Help them to see what you value them for – to appreciate their own qualities – and how they owe it to themselves to wait for the right person and the right time. It will be worth it.

I've got something to tell you . . .

'How can I tell Ben I don't want to see him any more?' It's easy, isn't it, to respond to this question in a supportive and practical way. 'How can I tell him I like somebody else?' This takes more careful thinking. 'How do I tell him that "somebody else" is another girl?' This may be more challenging than anything you have experienced before.

When you have already seen your daughter through several romances, of varying levels of seriousness, this one may come as a shock, to say the least. The young person that you thought you 'knew' suddenly shows a facet to her personality that is totally unexpected and alien. The temptation is to think that she is not the daughter you thought she was. This is, of course, not true. She is still 'yours', still the same person, still the same member of your family. She has merely taken a different turning off the road that you had envisaged for her. It might be a little rockier, but that's all! It is your role to make sure that she knows you are still there to help her to navigate.

It is a fact that teenagers inwardly question their sexuality and struggle to find what 'fits' them best. This struggle can be a painful one for some young people who cannot reconcile their feelings to what is regarded as 'normal'. As parents, we have grown to have expectations of our children in all aspects of life. We expect them to exhibit social behaviour that is acceptable;

we expect them to achieve their full educational potential; we expect them to develop personal and social skills that will help them to make their way in society. How much of this is expecting them to 'conform' to the traditional conventions of society that were relevant in our teenage years? It has taken a long time for our society to learn to accept other 'differences' within our midst – disability, gender and race equality. Why should a person's sexuality be any different?

There is a strong need for young people to know that we understand their feelings and are willing to help them through what is, inevitably, a confusing time for them. We have to be comfortable in helping them to explore or come to terms with how they feel about themselves. In doing so, we may also need our own support. Feel safe in the knowledge that you are not the first parent to be faced with this challenge; there are many local and national support groups, or you may even find unexpected reassurance from friends and family. Parents of gay and lesbian young people are a great 'listening ear'. They have heard all the worries, concerns, prejudices and anxieties before and have probably experienced them themselves.

Don't expect an easy journey. There will be times when doubts and fears come to mind – but these will always come as part of being a parent. In the long run you must be secure in the knowledge that your daughter will be with someone she cares for and who cares for her and that she has the confidence to deal with some of the difficult issues she may face. After all, not everybody she meets will be as understanding as parents are. Never close the conversations that need to be had, ask to hear the truth from your daughter, and make sure that she is happy to hear the truth from you. For more information and support see the relevant websites listed at the back of this book.

Sexual relationships Q&A

Q: My 13-year-old daughter says she has a boyfriend — isn't she too young?

A: It all depends on what your daughter means when she says that she has a boyfriend. Relationships with the opposite sex will blossom from puberty onwards; what is important is that your daughter has the tools both to deal with the attendant strong emotions and to say 'no' to the development of a sexual element at this early age. Parents often find it difficult to talk to their daughters about sex; try reading a down-to-earth leaflet for parents produced by Parentlineplus, entitled *Keeping your Teenager Safe: Talking about Relationships*. If you find that you need further support, consult their helpline at www.parentlineplus.org.uk.

My daughter's boyfriend is taking over her life

Q: My daughter has a boyfriend who has completely taken over her life. She doesn't see any of her school friends socially, which means that she now feels 'isolated' at school, and this has led to truanting. The school has been very understanding, but I am afraid that they will eventually lose patience. The teachers have given her a great deal of support, and she was set a lot of work to catch up on over the summer. I was hoping that the summer holiday would give time for her to reconnect with her friends, but instead it has made the position worse! She self-harms, which, coupled with the fact that she is incredibly emotional, makes trying to have a sensible conversation about any of the issues lead to shouting, slammed doors and her storming out of the house. She has now started her GCSE year (Year 11) and keeps trying to reassure me that she will work hard, but I have heard these promises before, and they have been broken every time. Any suggestions on how to handle this situation?

A: Try to engage external help in the form of counselling, as this is not really about your daughter's boyfriend, but rather about how she feels about herself and her life — her lack of self-love — and neither you nor she is going to be able to resolve this situation alone. How, though, can you make your daughter see a counsellor? Firstly, go to the school again, and talk about the issues that most concern you. You certainly need the school to adopt a tougher line with your daughter, in order to help support you — they should be less understanding about the truanting and more insistent upon her following the rules; if she truants, she should make up the time — she has to see that her actions have conse-quences. Does the school know about your daughter's self-harming? If not, you should tell them — some schools have a policy of not permitting pupils to be in school if they self-harm until they have a proper counselling course in place to support them and help them to recover. You need all the pressure you can find to bring to bear on your daughter to ensure that she sees a counsellor — sometimes the threat of not being allowed in school can be enough of a shock to make girls toe the line in this respect. In the past, you may have found yourself apologising for your daughter's behaviour to the school, and asking for their forgiveness and under-standing, and they may have taken their lead from you; now, however, is the time for firm boundaries, which your daughter will actually crave, and together you will be stronger. Moreover, the school may have some good ideas about potential counsellors experienced in dealing with teen-agers; failing this, ask your GP. Don't blame yourself

— teenagers are complex beings, and she needs someone who is trained to help her see why she is behaving in the way she is, and to help her address how she feels. This is worth investing in — and now.

Vampire books — harmless fantasy or an inappropriate subject?

Q: My 14-year-old daughter has just been given the book Marked by P. C. Cast (it's a vampire novel — she likes the Twilight series). I've just read it and don't like the fact it has some sexual content. Also, like some other vampire books, blood lust and sex are connected, and I think it's inappropriate for her age. I'm not sure how to deal with this, as someone else gave it to her. Am I being naive in assuming she won't understand the sexual references?

A: Discuss your concerns with your daughter. The book does have some bad language and sexual content but, rather like Buffy the Vampire Slayer, it's the combination of a high school setting and teenage preoccupations with the supernatural that makes it appealing to young readers, and many girls of your daughter's age are likely to be reading this type of book.

On the positive side, the book does contain a moral message about the inadvisability and dangers of casual sex, drink and drugs — but there is some titillation, too, and girls will be attracted to it because of the risqué nature of some of the references. It's similar to the issue of what girls need to be taught about sex and relationships. Ignorance is the most dangerous thing of all, and at least the book isn't presenting casual sex as 'cool'. Girls are interested in the emotional repercussions of becoming interested in the opposite sex and they will enjoy the vicarious thrill of the romantic episodes.

It is likely that many 14-year-olds will understand the sexual references, though younger girls might not and should probably be discouraged from reading it.

If the book was a gift from a family friend, perhaps let the buyer know of your reservations — especially as this is one of a series of six books and if they think the gift is a success, this might happen several more times! However, censorship is a difficult issue — and we can't protect our children from the realities of the world. We just have to educate them and communicate clearly and openly so they make their own choices as best they can.

I think my daughter and her boyfriend are getting serious

Q: *My daughter (aged 15+) has just started going out with her first boyfriend. Although we have discussed sex issues in the past, it has only been about Sexually Transmitted Infections (STIs). How do I broach a chat about sex in relation to her own ideas of how she might behave in a relationship? I don't want to embarrass her, but I feel it would be irresponsible not to speak to her.*

A: This is indeed a test of your courage. You could start by telling her it is not an easy conversation, as you do not want to invade her privacy, but that you love her, and each generation can at least consider the advice of the one before, even if they do not take it.

She will do what she and her boyfriend want to do — but if he is young, too, and you get the feeling that they are contemplating sex, you could point out that they might both prefer to wait — discuss in what other ways they can enjoy time together. If he is older, it is even more important to discuss why it is illegal for them to have sex, and be much more discouraging generally, as she is at risk of being persuaded by a more mature sexual partner. Do discuss the age of consent with her and ensure that she realises it is there as a child protection measure. It is helpful for her to know your views, as long as she also knows that you are not trying to control her. She may well share her own views, and such a discussion may increase her confidence in expressing them to him in a discussion.

Encourage her to think about the emotional issues that come with a romantic and sexual relationship, and how she and her boyfriend can protect themselves from the possible downsides (loss of freedom in deciding how to spend their time without reference to the other, likelihood of collapse of the romance as they each grow up, worry over pregnancy and possible disease, etc.) and think about the fun of romance without a full sexual relationship, which can have most of the advantages without the snags at this age.

Don't give them too much time alone together – parents have real responsibilities here. Warn her about the impact of alcohol on decision-making and that a large minority of pregnancies result from occasions when no sex was planned, but instead happened when one or both partners were a bit drunk. Her reputation matters here, too – other people respect someone who respects their own behaviour, and news spreads. Whatever the result of open discussions like this, you would be wise to be prepared and suggest they visit the Family Planning Association website (www.fpa.org.uk) or similar websites.

It sounds as though you have correctly realised that it is the way we all treat each other that matters. As such, your daughter should ensure she is making her decisions in the emotional context of not putting pressure on her boyfriend, or he on her, and that the two of them can together behave in ways that give them the greatest happiness in a sensible form, and do the least damage to each separately when things change for them in the future. Make sure you emphasise that she can always ask you for advice or support, however embarrassed she might be. You will have shown her that you love her enough to have this first conversation now, however embarrassed you were to start it.

Growing up

Your daughter may start her life as a bold, brave tomboy, as a shy sensitive soul or as a dancing princess. As she grows she may well be all of these and more. As she explores her potential, her enthusiasms and her capabilities, how will you help her value herself for who she is rather than who she thinks she ought to be?

To acquire the self esteem that is essential for her emotional health and success she needs your guidance to discover her strengths, whether they are academic or sporting, social or emotional. She needs your help to deal with the inevitable disappointments and failures. She needs your encouragement to take risks so she can become brave, resilient and realistic.

Alcohol and Drugs

Your daughter is likely to face social pressures as she matures, including being urged to drink alcohol and perhaps to take drugs. She is most likely to be able to make sensible, informed decisions if she has good self-esteem and a strong sense of self-worth. By setting a good example and by communicating frequently in a non-judgemental way you will give her the best chance of keeping herself safe and maintaining her personal integrity. The media is full of poor role models and of stories of teenagers' bad behaviour; by talking to her you can explain your concerns in a calm and loving way so that she will come to you first when she is worried or feeling pressured.

Teenagers and alcohol

Why has teenage drinking increased so dramatically – and, at times, so dangerously – in recent years? If it is because our children have low self-esteem, lack of social confidence or have some other deep-seated psychological issues, the underlying cause must be found and dealt with.

For the majority of teenage carousers, however, it isn't anything serious – it's just those ever-present favourite motivators for nearly all teenage behaviour, 'having a laugh', appearing 'cool' and being incapable of predicting consequences.

We can tell them until we are blue in the face that getting drunk is dangerous, causes road accidents (pedestrians as well as drivers), leads to people doing all sorts of things they'll be embarrassed about for a long time to come and for girls can often be a factor in rape or sexual assault, but they are unlikely to pay much attention.

As usual, the tactic that won't work is a lecture on irresponsible behaviour. Instead, try to think laterally:

- Do they want to have fun, be silly and let their hair down? Instead, how about a day at a theme park, laser tag, a visit to a racecourse or dog track, quad biking or abseiling?
- Do they want to feel adult and sophisticated? Instead, how about cocktails with all the trimmings but no alcohol? How about a group of parents hiring a disco for the kids? How about a party with great dance tracks and a punch that is rumoured to contain vodka? (Of course, it doesn't, but you wouldn't be the first parents to carry off that particular white lie!)

It is often suggested that allowing children a small amount of alcohol at home (the French wine and water model) can help to deglamorise later drinking at clubs. A good Personal, Social and Health Education (PSHE) programme at school should give teenagers plenty to think about as well as some hard information on the contents of alcopops and the potentially lethal combined effect of vodka and Red Bull, etc. If real shock tactics are called for, you could make them stay sober at a party where everyone else is drinking, or video them while under the influence themselves. It's not funny the next day.

Getting drunk is not a phenomenon that is new to the present generation and making mistakes is part of growing up. However, we must try to protect our youngsters against making mistakes that could affect their lives permanently.

Teenage parties and alcohol

Most parents are worried about their children coming into contact with drugs, but the real social evil is alcohol. With spirits retailing at less than £10 a bottle in supermarkets, most teenagers can afford to pick up a bottle with their pocket money. Fake IDs are routine, and there is usually an older teen around to effect the transaction. The prevalence of alcopops has taken away one of the greatest bars on teenage drinking – the taste. Most young teenagers don't like the taste of beer, wine or cider. Alcopops vary in their alcoholic content, but they appeal to those with a sweet tooth, go down like fizzy drinks and have become an entry level to drinking spirits. It is no surprise that teenage drinking is now a national problem.

The world of teenage parties and alcohol is one of the most difficult situations that parents face. Children will always try to play parents off against each other – 'So-and-so's parents let them, you are SO tight!' – and the consequence is that it is tempting for parents to default to the level of the most liberal of parents. It is important that parents establish good lines of communication between each other and that they are clear about a number of keys issues, namely:

- at what age alcohol will be available
- the amount and type of alcohol that will be provided
- what levels of supervision will be in place throughout a party

If alcohol is to be allowed at a party, limit access to wines and beers only (e.g. no spirits). Although alcopops, which are particularly popular with girls, blur the spirit/non-spirit divide, at least they are a 'measured' drink. A strong, active adult presence at all teenage parties is essential. 'Policing' duties range from excluding gate-crashers to being alert to 'smuggled in' illicit additional supplies of alcohol. A minimum of three adults at a ratio of one adult to ten teenagers should provide a good level of supervision and sufficient cover if anything goes wrong.

Alcohol is a normal part of adult society, and it is important that young people learn to drink responsibly. This skill is best taught in the home, with parents perhaps offering a glass of wine with a meal or when at a family gathering. Supervision is the key. The greatest dangers come when teenagers are given an opportunity to have access to alcohol – especially spirits – away from the home or behind closed doors.

Most importantly, parents should not underestimate the part that we play as role models to our children. Young people will pay more attention to what we do than to what we say.

Alcohol – how to spot if your child is drinking too much, the signs and how to tackle them

We should be under no illusions – alcohol can be extremely dangerous for children and teenagers, and you are right to be concerned if you think that your child is drinking. While a single glass of wine for a 16-year-old at a family dinner can help your children to understand the boundaries of social drinking, illicit binge drinking, especially of spirits, is damaging to a child's health, can be life-threatening and can lead to extremely risky behaviour. Figures vary, but it is estimated that up to 80 per cent of early sexual experiences occur under the influence of alcohol, and the vast majority of these experiences are subsequently regretted.

So what can you do to protect your daughter? The first thing, of course, is to know if she is drinking and to do this you need to be very aware of where she is at all times. If she is out with friends, then always make sure that you see her on her return and engage her in conversation. If she smells of alcohol, or strongly of mints or of perfume, then you are right to be suspicious. Keep her talking and you will be able to see if there is any difference in her behaviour – is she chattier or more volatile than usual? If you are worried that you don't know whether your child is drinking too much, then remember this: the safest approach is that any unsupervised alcohol is too much.

Don't be naive about parties, even those supervised by other parents. Children – teenagers especially, and even the most law-abiding and delightful ones – need to try to break the rules and are extraordinarily ingenious when it comes to doing so. Drink can easily be smuggled into houses, and innocent-looking water bottles can easily contain vodka. Parties with sleepovers usually mean that parents go to bed before their charges, and it is then that the hidden stash of wine or spirits can appear. Share your concerns with the people supervising the party, talk to your daughter to set out your expectations and follow this up. If you are in any doubt about the party, put your foot down – hard though this will be – and weather the storm (but replace it with something else amazing to do instead with you and your family).

Talking to your daughter about alcohol is really important and – like talking about sex – is best introduced from an early age as part of an ongoing conversation about what is right and what is wrong in life. (Do make it clear you are talking about drinking alcohol, though – you might send some rather contradictory messages, otherwise!) Expressing disapproval or concern over drunken behaviour is a good way of starting to get the message across to young children that alcohol can lead people to do things that make them look silly. As children grow older, the key to effective discussion is an open relationship in which you allow your child or teenager to talk comfortably to you. Admittedly, this is easier said than done, but the secret to this is to listen, listen, listen and to help your daughter to reach conclusions by talking through her thoughts. Children are going to make mistakes – statistics show that they are likely to try alcohol and overindulge before the age of 18 on at least one occasion – and if this can be turned into a learning experience, then this is all to the good.

Of course, to repeat an important message to parents, you are an extremely important role model for your daughter. She needs to see sensible behaviour from you in this respect if you are to have any chance of guiding her actions – she will do as you do, not just as you say . . .

Don't be afraid to seek help if you suspect that your daughter is drinking too much. If you want to know more, a useful starting point is www.drinkaware.co.uk, which has an excellent section on facts about alcohol, as well as a really useful page on how to introduce the topic with your children, and how to follow it through.

Teenagers and drugs

It is every parent's nightmare that their daughter will take drugs. Drugs are out there and readily available. As adults, we have the benefit of our own experiences and hindsight to make informed choices about what we do; children do not yet have this. It is therefore vital that young people are educated about the effects and dangers of drugs. Being authoritarian and judgmental by telling your daughter what she should and should not do tends to be ineffective. What she needs are the real facts so that she can make informed and, hopefully, safe and sensible choices.

To help your daughter to make the right decisions, she needs open communication, positive role modelling and facts.

What is meant by 'drugs'?

Drugs are chemicals or substances that change the way in which our bodies work. You should be aware of the effects and risks for your daughter if she uses aerosols, alcohol, anabolic steroids, cannabis, cocaine, crack, ecstasy, gases, glues, GHB, heroin, Ketamine, LSD, Magic Mushrooms, meow meow, poppers, Speed, tobacco or tranquillisers.

Why would she take drugs?

The motivations for taking drugs vary and have a great deal to do with the user's relationship with others around them. Here is a list of possible reasons for taking drugs:

- Your daughter may be bored and looking for some excitement or experimentation.
- She may succumb to peer pressure. 'Take these to make you feel good' or 'You will have a better time if you take them.'
- Your daughter might be persuaded if she believes not to do so would lose her friends, especially a boyfriend.
- Some people believe that drugs will make them think better or make them more popular; others are just curious and think one try won't hurt them.
- Many teenagers believe that drugs will solve their problems, or at least allow them to escape from them. They might want to escape emotional upset; to feel less anxious; to avoid thinking about things or making decisions.
- There may be more physical reasons, such as blocking out pain or just the pleasure of the 'buzz'.
- Drugs can also be used to increase or reduce energy levels or to help people relax.

GROWING UP

What are the warning signs?
Changes in personality:
Unexpected mood swings, overly tired or hyperactive, withdrawn or rebellious behaviour, narrow attitude to problems and solutions.

Changes at home:
Loss of interest in family activities, withdrawal from responsibility, sudden increase or decrease in appetite, money or valuable items disappearing, secretive or suspicious behaviour.

Changes at school:
General bad attitude, drop in grades and interest, truancy.

Changes in physical appearance:
Lack of general hygiene, greasy hair, odd smell, spots, rashes, sores, pale and gaunt, yellow teeth, wearing sunglasses, long sleeves or coats at inappropriate times.

Physical evidence:
Cigarettes, rolling paper, foil, empty small plastic bags, burnt or bent spoons, strange short phone calls at odd hours, lies about activities, appearance of new and 'unsuitable' friends.

What should a parent do?
First of all, be aware that some of the signs can also be indicative of emotional problems and individually they could be attributed to simply being a teenager. So, first, talk to your daughter. The best approach is to explain that you think she might have problems and that you want to help. Reassure her that she is not in trouble, as this will inevitably lead to denial and unwillingness to talk.

Who else can help?
You cannot deal with this alone, and too many parents are worried about what other people might think. You will need

help, advice, information and support and this will involve 'outsiders'. Approach your family doctor and contact your daughter's school. There are websites listed at the back of this book that may prove useful.

Caffeine abuse and addiction

Students keeping themselves awake with black coffee or Pro Plus is not a new issue. But is the increasing popularity and availability of high-caffeine colas and so-called 'energy' drinks causing ever-younger girls to indulge? What are the signs to look out for and what can you do to help? The consumption of caffeine may lead to teenagers experiencing an energy boost and increased mental alertness, but overconsumption can lead to disrupted sleeping patterns, irritability and 'caffeine lows' during the day. Parents should:

- Realise that some young people may choose to take stimulants while revising late in the evening or prior to examinations in order to boost their alertness.
- Be aware of the pressure points in your daughter's homework, study and examination timetables so you can monitor her wellbeing.
- Try to reinforce messages from schools that pupils should have sensible sleeping hours, a healthy balanced diet and regular study breaks.

If you are concerned about caffeine abuse, watch out for the following:

- Is her behaviour erratic and/or hyperactive?
- Is she suffering from an unusual number of headaches, irritability or lack of concentration? These are all signs of caffeine withdrawal.
- Is she drinking increasing or excessive amounts of fizzy drinks, such as colas and Red Bull?

What to do if you see signs of caffeine abuse:

- Offer your daughter alternatives to the drinks she is consuming.
- Talk to her school to see if they are seeing the same signs. They will be able to reassure you if there is not a problem or step in to help if there is, perhaps providing access to independent advice or a counsellor, should it prove necessary.
- Make sure she knows the facts. Younger girls can be persuaded into trying tablets such as Pro Plus and high-caffeine drinks without realising they can do any harm. They will know that it is not illegal and may therefore assume there is no danger. Explain that excess caffeine can cause behavioural changes and can ultimately lead to addiction.

If you are concerned about your daughter's stress levels, encourage her to try some of the following solutions:

- Recognise her symptoms of stress. If she is getting stressed, talking – with relatives, friends, a Head of Year, tutor or the school nurse – will help to put things in perspective and help her to decide on a course of action.
- Good nutrition will aid the body's mechanisms for coping with stress. Drink plenty of water.
- Get enough sleep. Sleep is vital for wellbeing.
- Physical activity is a good way to release the stress hormones from her body. She could try a stretching routine, swim, cycle, dance or take a walk.

The medical facts:

While caffeine can have beneficial effects in terms of increased alertness and an ability to tolerate sleep deprivation (the reason many people use it during exam periods as an aid to revision), higher doses can result in a number of adverse effects, including increased nervousness, anxiety, insomnia, palpitations, tremors, headaches and mild confusion, which would certainly have an adverse effect on exam performance. While caffeine use is, of course, quite legal, it is important to make girls aware of the problems that excess caffeine may cause. In particular, many people do not realise the high caffeine content present in a number of common beverages and stimulant drinks that are heavily advertised as substances to enhance general performance. As a result, awareness and education about the effects of caffeine are extremely important, and these are areas that teachers may well discuss while advising their pupils on how to prepare for examinations, as well as in Personal, Social and Health Education (PSHE) sessions.

Alcohol and drugs Q&A

Is my daughter secretly drinking?
Q: I have found an opened bottle of wine in my daughter's bedroom (three-quarters of the bottle had been drunk). She is 14 years old — what should I do?

A: It is important that you do not rush to punish your daughter before you have had a calm, honest conversation. You could tell her that you found the bottle and ask her to explain. Ask her to tell you about how, when, where and with whom she drinks. Don't accuse her, for it is possible that she was an unwilling bystander and has left the bottle for you to find as a signal for help on how she can handle this.

Most likely, however, she will have been drinking and you will want to show both your concern and disapproval. You need to acknowledge that at some point she would start to drink alcohol but that you believe she is too young and that lying to or deceiving you undermines your relationship.

The danger of stern punishment is that it can lead to her 'staying at friends' homes' more and more frequently, and you will have little idea of how she is actually behaving. Hopefully, you can continue good communication with your daughter even after you've expressed your disappointment over her drinking and why this causes you to worry about her safety.

How do I stop my daughter drinking?

Q: *I grounded my daughter for a month for drinking alcohol. The grounding finished today and I let her out with her friends. I got a call from the police tonight, as they had arrested my daughter for being drunk and disorderly. I was so ashamed. She was also sick in the van and I have to pay the cleaning bill. I can't believe she has done this again after promising she wouldn't, never mind the fact it's on her first night out after being grounded. What can I do this time? I'm at my wits' end.*

A: Young women's drinking habits are certainly a cause for concern, and it is understandable how worried you must be. Grounding your daughter hasn't worked, so a different approach is necessary. Although it is a relatively easy and tempting punishment, grounding pushes her away. She will be angry with you for what she thinks she is missing out on and may want to rebel further. Instead, you need her to reflect on her behaviour. You don't say how old your daughter is, but even if she is in her late teens, she should be learning to drink responsibly.

The first step is for you to speak with her. Try to remain calm and explain why you are so concerned about her apparent inability to control her drinking. Remind her of how vulnerable she is when she is out of control while under the influence of alcohol. Tell her what could happen to her and that this is why you are so desperately worried about her behaviour. Emphasise your fears for her safety, rather than your disgust and embarrassment at her lack of control. Keep talking to her, listen to her and make it easy for her to come home to you, even if drunk. Negotiate boundaries — for instance, she should always keep you informed about whom she goes out with, where she is going and you should agree a time when she will come home.

Just as you cannot make a young child eat, you cannot control a teenager. Your aim should be to enable her to learn to control herself. Be interested in her friends and social life without being too critical — you don't want her to 'go underground' by lying to you. Suggest that your daughter take a look at the alcohol section on talktofrank. com, a website aimed at teenagers rather than their parents. Finally, remember that growing up involves making mistakes and, hopefully, learning from them.

Food and diet

Food is an emotional issue. It is important to recognise whether your daughter's faddy or fussy eating could develop into anorexia or bulimia. Is she obsessed with food or just trying to have a healthy diet?

Girls and food

Young girls

Children, and girls in particular, have a tendency to copy others. Because of this, eating as a family, including at school, encourages them to eat well. Some young children can be faddy eaters and, although you should tell your daughter's school if she is vegetarian or has any significant food issues, she may well feel more confident to try new foods away from any home tensions.

It is important that the kitchen table is not a battleground, and there are several helpful books and websites that offer strategies for encouraging healthy eating – try *Healthy Eating for Kids* by Anita Bean or www.eatwell.gov.uk/agesandstages/children. If your daughter is aware that family members are unhappy with their body or with hers, she may fall into bad eating habits. The media's obsession with body image means it is important that your daughter gets the right message about food from home.

Growing children need a balanced diet that includes carbo-hydrates and fats in order to form a healthy body, and at various stages a little body fat is natural. However, childhood obesity is a significant concern, and an overweight child is setting up health problems for her future.

Teenagers

During the teenage years, girls and food can be a strange combi-nation. Your daughter spends many hours in school, so it is important that what is provided is both what she needs and what she wants. Most schools are sensitive to the dangers of eating problems and they work hard to provide interesting, healthy food. If you're providing packed lunches, you should cater for your daughter's preferences but also ensure that her meal is balanced and nutritious.

Your daughter is growing fast and studying hard and needs sustenance. Breakfast is vital, whether eaten at home or on arrival at school. Local shops or school tuck shops should supplement main meals, not replace them. A constant supply of chilled water helps everyone to rehydrate and concentrate. But while this is easy to say, girls' relationships with food can be fraught with potential problems. An overweight girl can be bullied and may become very unhappy; the most popular girl is often the one with the best figure and she is likely to be slim. Most girls will diet at some stage during their school lives. Bombarded by images of super-skinny celebrities, your daughter may equate size with success, fame and happiness. For her, puppy fat is not a natural part of growing up but an unnecessary evil. Playground crazes may give way to diet fads and calorie counting. Even school lessons on healthy eating can rebound, if once she is aware of fats and carbohydrates, she decides to avoid them, thus cutting out necessary nutrients.

Schools are very aware of the importance of a healthy diet and as they see your daughter each day, they will keep an eye on her. It really is quite simple: a growing girl needs sufficient nutritious food of a high quality to give her the energy she needs. If your daughter doesn't eat well, she won't be able to work or play to her full potential.

Eating disorders

I need information. Where do I start?
There is a vast amount of information available on all types of eating disorders, such as anorexia and bulimia. There are

7 million references on Google alone, numerous articles in magazines, examples in films and on TV, and your daughter will know a great deal about them. One of the best websites is www.b-eat.co.uk. It contains a wealth of information and some simple but basic statements that will help you to understand whether your daughter is a faddy eater or on a relatively harmless diet or if she actually has an eating disorder. Here are some helpful tips for concerned parents, taken from the b-eat website:

- *Neither anorexia nor bulimia is a dieting craze.*
- *An eating disorder is not attention-seeking.*
- *An eating disorder is serious.*
- *An eating disorder is an illness.*
- *Eating disorders can be beaten.*

What is an eating disorder?

Both food and eating play a very important part in our lives. It is not unusual to experiment with different eating habits – for example, you may have decided to become a vegetarian or tried changing your diet to improve your health. However, some eating patterns can be damaging.

Problems can begin to emerge when food is used to cope with times of boredom, anxiety, anger, loneliness, shame or sadness. Food becomes a problem when it is used as a crutch to help cope with painful situations or feelings, or to relieve stress. Occasionally, this can happen without the individual even realising it.

If this is how you deal with emotions and you are unhappy about it, then you should try to talk to someone whom you trust. It is unlikely that an eating disorder will result from a single cause. It is much more likely to result from a combination of many factors, events, or pressures that lead to feelings of an inability to cope. These can include: low self-esteem, family relationships, problems with friends, the death of someone special, problems at school, college or university, lack of confidence or sexual or emotional abuse.

People with eating disorders often say that the eating disorder is the only way they feel in control of their life. However, as time goes on, it isn't really you who is in control, it is the eating disorder.

Who do eating disorders affect and when?

Anyone can develop an eating disorder, regardless of age, sex or cultural or racial background, although the people most likely to be affected tend to be young women, particularly between the ages of 15 to 25.

The attitude of other family members towards food can have an impact. A key person – such as a parent or relative – may unwittingly influence other family members through his or her attitude to food. In situations in which there are high academic expectations, family issues or social pressures, your daughter may focus on food and eating as a way of coping with these stresses.

Eating disorders are occasionally triggered by a traumatic event, such as bereavement, bullying or abuse, family upheaval (such as divorce), long-term illness or concerns about sexuality. Someone with a long-term illness or disability, such as diabetes, depression, blindness or deafness, may also experience eating problems.

How will I know if anything is wrong?

As with all teenage girls, speak with your daughter about everything. Keep an eye on her weight. There is a difference between faddy diets and eating disorders. There can be many signs: if your daughter has lost a great deal of weight quickly and wants to lose more; if she is hiding under layers of clothes; if she hides food or goes immediately to the bathroom after eating.

What do I do if I suspect my daughter has an eating disorder?

Talk to her but tread carefully and do not accuse her straight away. Seek help and advice, especially from your GP and the school.

Thoughts from a Head — Children and food — the importance of a good meal

Prue Leith wasn't pulling any punches when she used her valedictory speech as chair of the School Food Trust to criticise parents for allowing their children to have 'all-the-chips-you-can eat for a pound' rather than paying for a healthy school meal. Acknowledging that she had underestimated the challenge the Trust faced to influence children's attitude to food, she blamed parents for infecting their children with poor eating habits and lamented the decline in family meals around a table. She also turned her guns on the producers of crisps and chocolate for directing their huge marketing budgets at children and selling them junk.

This was a perfect example of how we cannot educate in a vacuum. Since Jamie Oliver's crusade in 2005, rigorous nutritional standards have been introduced and the quality of school dinners has risen. But however much effort schools make to produce appetising food and to educate young people about a balanced diet, promoting healthy eating for kids will be a struggle if the home has not provided a good foundation.

Family meal times are of central importance, not just to appreciate well-prepared, tasty food, but for the central socialising role that coming together for a meal plays in developing social abilities, such as conversing with confidence, listening and having meaningful discussion. Being around food in the home naturally teaches children a great deal about shared responsibility: about helping to cook, lay and clear the table and wash up; about noticing the needs of others so passing the jug of water or the salt.

Miss Leith did not spare schools, either, and she berated Head Teachers and governing bodies for their lack of firm commitment to quality food served in their schools. But what does it mean to be committed? Commitment means employing a catering manager who understands what good food is and is prepared to encourage creativity in her chefs; it means recruiting and training chefs who are concerned enough to make sure that the students are enjoying their food and seeking feedback about different menus; it means ensuring that there is enough variety and choice for pupils to have a balanced meal and it also means making sure that good quality ingredients are used and presentation is appetising. While it is good to involve students in discussion about food and to listen to their feedback, it is important to retain professional responsibility to educate and to broaden pupils' horizons about how they might try new and healthy foods, rather than simply to pander to their whims.

Some of you may have bitter memories of your own school food: of being made to eat everything on your plate, of gristle, boiled cabbage, overcooked pig's liver and semolina that made you retch. But the history of food in this country over the past half century is one of two halves. One half began when people started to go abroad en masse and, as a result, began incorporating foreign influences to make food much more interesting. The other is of processed and fast foods; snacking; eating while watching TV; eating in the street; fads; allergies and a burgeoning problem with obesity. Miss Leith believes teaching children to actually *like* good food is as important to their future success as being literate or numerate. In the interests of building a civilised society, she may be right.

Food Q&A

Q: My daughter is not happy with her body. She thinks she is fat and talks about going on a diet. How can I stop her becoming anorexic?

A: Firstly, don't panic. Many, if not most, girls lack confidence. They are bombarded with retouched pictures of seemingly perfect women in magazines and can easily feel inadequate. Ask yourself if she is picking up similar dissatisfaction from you; it is important that she feels you think she is lovely. Agree to help her to eat healthily and don't try to 'feed her up' if you think she is dieting too hard. Young women today are very aware of the importance of a healthy lifestyle, so by offering to help her achieve this, you will give her good habits.

Is my vegetarian daughter getting enough protein?
Q: My daughter has just become a vegetarian, and no longer eats meat, poultry or fish, but she is still growing. How I can I make sure she gets enough protein?

A: The proportion of girls choosing a vegetarian diet rises to around 10 per cent of girls in the 15 to 18 age group, so you are not alone in asking this important question. Your daughter's whole diet and nutritional intake will influence her current and future health. There is a growing body of evidence for links between nutrition and academic and sporting performance, and between nutrition and behaviour and mood. It is important that she learns about healthy vegetarian choices, so that she is able to obtain adequate protein and other essential nutrients in her diet as an adult.

You mentioned that your daughter needs protein for

growth, but she also needs it for just about every process in her body. Proteins are needed for muscle contraction, immunity and the transmission of nerve impulses. They also provide structure for skin and bone. Protein from food is broken down in the body into amino acids. The body must obtain a full spectrum of these, and fortunately vegetarian diets can easily provide them. While milk, cheese and eggs provide the full range of amino acids, many plant sources of protein, such as pulses and grains, do not individually provide the full range. Combining these plant proteins leads to a full spectrum of protein. Therefore, your daughter needs to eat a good variety of foods containing protein. Soya, quinoa and hemp seeds each provide the full spectrum of amino acids, so these are high quality proteins on their own.

You should try to help your daughter to obtain the following in her diet: a variety of nuts (walnuts, brazil nuts, almonds, pine nuts, cashews) and seeds (sunflower, pumpkin, sesame and linseed); a variety of pulses, known as legumes (chickpeas, lentils, split peas, kidney beans, black-eyed beans, butter beans, pinto beans, cannellini beans, haricot beans, soya beans and soya products, such as tofu); a variety of grain products (wheat, rye, barley and quinoa); eggs; dairy products, such as those from cow's milk: for example yoghurt or cheese (hard and soft); goat's and ewe's milk products, such as feta cheese. Do note, however, that cheese, while a very good source of protein, can also provide high levels of saturated fats if eaten in large quantities.

You may find that initially, as you get used to cooking without meat, poultry or fish, cooking becomes more time-consuming. You should not be tempted to rely too much on processed meat-replacement items. Meat substitutes such as vege-mince and Quorn are often overused as protein sources. These are very highly processed products, and the details of the manufacturing processes reveal how far the finished product is from the raw ingredients. Because of this, meals should generally be prepared from scratch — which is, of course, healthier anyway. A well-planned vegetarian diet is very healthy; it's even worth encouraging other members of the family to have 'veggie days'. In fact, some argue that vegetarianism is good for the planet by being a 'green' choice!

How do I help my overweight daughter?

Q: *My older daughter has become very tubby, not just a bit overweight. She wolfs down her dinner long before the rest of us are even partway through ours, and then seems to still be hungry, getting toast, cereal, etc., through the evening. My younger daughter is quite slim, athletic and has a boyfriend and lots of other friends. I am so worried that my older daughter is comfort eating and hiding something from me. She appears happy enough in herself and talks to me about her friends and what she has done during the day. I have dropped hints about balanced diets and exercise, but she has lost interest in all the activities she used to love, like horse riding, cadets, swimming and walking. Should I tell her straight out that she is getting fat?*

A: Please don't tell your daughter you think she's fat. If she's comfort eating, it won't help as she will feel criticised and have an even greater need to comfort eat. It might also drive her to try to hide her eating, which could lead to bulimia.

Try discussing her eating and exercise rather than her size. Girls can be very sensitive about body size and need to feel that they are loved by their parents, no matter what size and shape they are. However, it is perfectly legitimate in a teenager's eyes for their parents to be concerned about their health, even though they may seem dismissive of it. It is possible there is a medical reason for your daughter's increased hunger — so you could suggest a visit to the doctor. In a quiet moment you could ask straight out if there is anything she is anxious about.

Exercise can be tackled in the same way, initially by just expressing that you've noticed she has lost interest in a lot of things she previously enjoyed. It may simply be that she has outgrown them, but it would be safe for you to express concern that she isn't getting a lot of exercise and that this isn't good for her health. Just knowing that you have noticed and care may well be all it takes for your daughter to address the issue herself or to open up to you a bit more, if necessary.

Girls and eating — your questions answered

Q: I am worried that my daughter is not eating properly. She is 15 and goes to boarding school, so it is difficult for me to keep an eye on her eating habits. She seems to have lost quite a lot of weight, and during the most recent holidays she found numerous excuses not to eat in front of me. Having suffered from anorexia myself when I was a similar age, I am suspicious. Although my anorexia could be attributed to an unhappy childhood, I have tried my best to provide a secure and happy home for her.

My question is, can anorexia be inherited, and will one's children be more susceptible to this addictive form of behaviour, despite a parent's efforts? What can I do to try to help, without making the problem worse?

A: Have you tried discussing your concerns with your daughter? It's important that she understands why you are worried. If you don't find her response reassuring, you should talk to the Head of Boarding at her school. They will have a great deal of experience that they can draw on and will be able to carefully monitor your daughter during term time.

On the website www.MyDaughter.co.uk, there are a

number of articles, queries and FAQs that relate to eating disorders. Enter 'anorexia' in the search box to read these.

While your own experience is understandably making you feel responsible, it's vital for you to remember that eating disorders, such as anorexia are mental illnesses, not physical ones. Therefore, it requires the aid of professionals, such as your GP — you and your daughter are not alone.

Q: *I have put down my daughter's name for an all girls' day school with a very good reputation, but I have been told by another parent that they have a long table set aside for girls who have eating disorders, so the staff can watch what they eat. While I am sure this is being done with the best of intentions, I am now becoming very concerned about sending her there because of this. Surely being singled out in this way makes the girls more susceptible to teasing and to the scrutiny of other girls, when these girls probably have a low self-image in the first place. If anything, I would think that such an emphasis would make the problem worse rather than better. I also think that if girls are determined not to eat, they will find a way of hiding or disposing of the food, no matter who is watching. Do you think I am right to be worried about this issue? I am concerned because I do have reason to believe that she may be placed on such a table.*

A: It is quite understandable why you are worried. You must approach the school you have selected for your daughter so that it can explain or deny what this parent has told you. Girls with eating disorders can find eating in public situations very stressful and sometimes allocating a separate table for them is a sensitive and helpful solution. Another factor is that some girls who eat 'normally' can be impressed by those who seem to be on 'successful diets', so separating these groups may be advisable.

You imply you have reason to believe your daughter has issues with eating. Don't hesitate to seek professional help, initially via your GP, if you need it

Q: I think my daughter may be anorexic. What should I do?

A: If you have noticed that your daughter is eating much less, or if she is avoiding eating altogether, then you probably have reason to be on alert. If she seems much thinner, then again, you are right to be concerned. Disordered eating is often the first step towards an eating disorder, and the sooner you act, the better informed and prepared you — and she — will be. The single most important piece of advice to give, however, is not to think that you will solve this yourself. An eating disorder such as anorexia is a mental illness, and you need a professional to help you gain objectivity. Contact an organisation such as b-eat — www.b-eat.co.uk. They have excellent resources and advice.

Anorexia in the family
Q: I'm very worried about my granddaughter. She has anorexia and my daughter, who is trying hard to help her, is hardly coping.

A: The first thing to do is reassure your daughter that you don't view her as a failure as a mother because of this. She needs lots of support with this problem, as does your granddaughter. Your daughter also needs to know that she is not alone in this situation.

If your daughter is not coping, specialist help is the key. It is highly likely that part of the specialist treatment will involve family therapy. At this point, parents and, in particular, mothers, will feel that they can cope better and feel supported. Through your granddaughter's school and specialist hospital unit, her mother should be able to make contact with other parents of children suffering from eating disorders, and sharing concerns with one another is most therapeutic. Schools often know of other mothers who have been down this route and got through the problem and who have offered to be referred to other parents who might need support. Tell your daughter to try asking the school specifically for this kind of contact and not to feel at all embarrassed about it.

For your granddaughter:

- The first port of call is the family GP, who is the best conduit for specialist help. Your daughter may already have done this.
- If anorexia has been formally diagnosed, then your granddaughter will be referred to an eating disorders clinic, probably attached to a hospital, where lots of help and advice will be on hand. Your granddaughter will probably be reluctant about this initially, and will need lots of love and persuasion that this is in her best interests.
- If she has accepted that she has a problem, she will be ready to be treated. If she has not, things will be much harder and the doctor again will be able to advise. Much will depend on the extent of the problem at this stage, and whether there has been a diagnosis. But think positive. Help is at hand.

Self-esteem

Strong self-esteem is vital for a child to be happy and successful. But how can you help your daughter develop hers? Girls are all too inclined to compare themselves unfavourably with the idealised pictures they see in the media and with their peers – with the media's portrayal of successful, 'perfect' women it's hardly surprising. Your daughter will, at some stage, almost certainly have anxieties about her appearance or her talents and abilities. If she has low self-esteem it will affect her in many ways – if she doesn't feel good about herself she will find it hard to handle life's inevitable challenges. Even the most outwardly confident girl may have inner doubts and find it difficult to handle disappointments or failure. By giving her praise when it's deserved, by focusing on her rather than making comparisons with others and by reassuring her of your unconditional love, you will help your daughter grow into a self-assured and happy young woman.

Self-esteem matters

What makes a person successful? Good A level results or a good degree? Looking stylish? Earning lots of money? There is a long list of things you might consider essential for success in life, but when you think of adults who are truly successful, you realise that there is a far more important credential: strong self-esteem.

It is easy to confuse self-esteem with confidence and to think that a girl who is outwardly bubbly, bright and engaging automatically has high self-esteem, but this does not necessarily follow. Sometimes outward appearances mask an inner fragility that can crumble at the first challenge. People with high self-esteem are comfortable within themselves and can cope with failure. They evaluate situations in which they have not performed well and look to build on the experience, becoming stronger as a result.

What every parent wants for their daughter is that she is able to cope with life's challenges. Therefore, it is important to work to build and maintain self-esteem throughout your daughter's life, both at home and at school.

Adolescence is a time when many girls suffer from low self-esteem. This can explain their challenging behaviour and temporary personality changes. As a parent, you can play a vital part at this stage by:

- Focusing on the positive: praise her whenever you can; tell her when she is doing well; reassure her about her appearance and achievements.
- Avoiding making comparisons: she is becoming her own individual self; help her to recover from any mistakes she makes.
- Be consistent in all interactions: set clear boundaries and stick to them; don't 'sweat the small stuff'; choose your battles.
- Make your daughter feel good about herself; she may be able to transfer this 'feel-good' factor to other parts of her life Challenges can help raise self-esteem. The important thing is to work with your daughter, and to tackle any specific existing issues head on.

Handbags and glad rags — being 'in' with the in crowd

Do you worry that your daughter suddenly seems preoccupied with her physical appearance, agonising over how attractive she is?

Is she measuring herself unrealistically against the norms of physical attractiveness within our society? Is she comparing herself against the society-led impossibility of willowy beauty, requiring her to be extremely thin? Have clothes become a very hot issue – does she have to have Ugg boots and the Jack Wills top or she won't be able to hold up her head in public? Is she experimenting with make-up in a way you find hard to accept? Why does she have this sudden apparent fixation with her looks?

Adolescent girls are often trying to contend with two apparently conflicting impulses: they want to be independent individuals (and certainly have independent views that may differ from those of their family), while, at the same time, they want to conform and not stand out from their peers. When they're not in school uniform, they are still in 'uniform', and may agonise over what to wear to the school disco, or on the school's charity fund-raising 'own clothes' day or on the last day of the Christmas term. Strangely, they are searching for an identity and trying to work out who they are, but one of the side effects of this is a tendency to become imitative; they know who the 'cool' crowd is, the attractive girls to whom others aspire, and they often want to look like them, dress like them, speak and act like them. Their sense of self-worth can depend on how effectively they manage to do so. Your daughter may also feel considerable pressure to enthuse about the same things as others do (regardless of what she thinks and feels), whether that's a type of music, a film or the desirability of a particular celebrity.

How do you communicate to your daughter that her value is not dependent on what she looks like or what she owns or wears?

Firstly, try not to be dismissive of her concerns. How well can you remember what it felt like to be her age and to feel the same pressure to be like everyone else? The labels and fashions may have changed, but the principle remains constant. If this is important to her, you may need to accept that – while at the same time encouraging her to be realistic about how much can be spent on such 'indispensable' items. If she wants to choose specific items of clothing for birthday and Christmas presents, or for special treats, and this will give her pleasure, you may need to go with this, even if the items chosen are not necessarily to your taste!

Secondly, it is important to encourage her to look beyond the surface of things and not to equate certain looks, clothing or behaviour with all that is desirable. Consider what characteristics she values in those she cares about and ensure she appreciates that the superficial can be meaningless or even misleading: physical appearance tells us very little about a person and what counts is something far more substantial. Ensure that your daughter is aware of the elements of her personality that make her special and are especially precious to those who love her, stressing that these values go far beyond how she looks.

Most of us do care how we look, and we feel better about ourselves if we feel that we look our best – this isn't just about being attractive to or pleasing others. An interest in our physical appearance and a desire to look good isn't something that's confined to adolescents. However, a fixation on appearance may be a particular cause of angst at certain times in your daughter's life. Help her to find the balance and to recognise that what we look like is only one (small) part of the picture.

The beauty myth — girls under pressure to be 'beautiful'

In light of constant press reports claiming that size-zero diets are 'ruining girls' health', how can parents help girls to maintain their self-esteem in the face of pressure to be 'beautiful' in the narrowest celebrity sense?

How can we encourage our daughters to see that healthy self-esteem is certainly more than skin deep, and that our value is not to be measured by our physicality? We have to accept that today our daughters are bombarded with images of a very specific and, many feel, distorted concept of beauty, which can make just about all of us feel inadequate. How many different brands of expensive perfume are there, and why does each need to be promoted with images of very slim, young and impossibly beautiful men and women romantically intertwined? If this is the accepted concept of beauty in our society, it is an unattainable ideal for almost every girl and woman who sees it on TV or in glossy magazines.

It is a natural human trait to wish to be attractive, and a huge industry has been born out of this. While this industry is aimed at both men and women, the brunt is felt most strongly by women. Perfume, cosmetics and beauty aids of every description are promoted wherever we look, and for young girls who are going through the sometimes painful process of deciding who they are and exactly what they are worth, these ubiquitous images selected to promote beauty products can be unhelpful.

Firstly, consider what we can say and do to encourage our daughters to feel good about themselves, and to recognise that this does not depend on superficial appearances. Indiscriminate praise tends not to have significant impact, but giving praise for specific accomplishments and positive elements of our personality can reinforce the message parents would hope to promote – that our self-worth is bound up with who we are and not what we look like.

Secondly, if your daughter is supported to try something new that she has to work at, but in which she ultimately achieves a measure of success, this can help her to feel capable. If your daughter is confident of your care for her, and the warmth and affection of others, this will show her that she is lovable. Positive self-esteem requires our recognition that we are both capable and lovable. It is good to receive a compliment that relates to how we look, but think about the compliments you offer your daughter that connect with what she has achieved or the positive qualities she has – enthusiasm, sensitivity, thoughtfulness or energy, perhaps. Tell your daughter she *is* beautiful, but ensure that she understands what that means and exactly where her beauty lies by being specific and positive.

The emotional wellbeing of girls in a celebrity culture

Around half of girls aged 7–21 believe that the pressure to look attractive is the most negative part of being female, and of those who have been on a strict diet, 66% claimed it was because of the media portrayal of women.[1] It is interesting to chart how the 'accepted' female form has developed over the last century. Marilyn Monroe was the epitome of a 1950s pin-up and reflected the average shape and weight of women at the time (about 60kg/9.4 stone). In the 1970s and 1980s we saw the 'ideal' woman as tall, thin, with highly toned muscle and an average weight of 56kg/8.8 stone. The 'ideal weight' of celebrities continued to fall, until we are now faced with the unnatural combination of narrow hips and large breasts with 'optimum' weights hitting 45.5kg/7.2 stone. With such unrealistic modern expectations, it is no wonder that, from a very young age, girls struggle with self-image and self-esteem.

The world of celebrity culture will continue to evolve of its own volition, but the most important thing for schools and parents is to bridge the gap between real life and the falsity of the media. One example of bridging such a gap is the experience of a group of 14–16-year-old girls who were shown the short film *Evolution*.[2] The film showed how a 'real girl' is transformed for a photoshoot. They were shocked at the amount of airbrushing and other 'tricks of the trade' that were employed during the process. It was then possible to get the girls to look with fresh eyes at advertising. Once their eyes were opened, they were able to get a sense that what they were seeing was not necessarily 'real'.

What can we do to support girls through this turbulent time? Encouraging and developing self-esteem, along with educating

---

1 Girlguiding UK, Girls' Attitudes Survey 2010
2 *Evolution*, Dove's Campaign for Real Beauty (www.*campaignforrealbeauty*.com).

them about how the media portrays images of celebrities, is key to ensuring girls have a realistic understanding of what constitutes 'normal'. However, it is becoming increasingly difficult to do this as celebrities themselves are targeted by the media for being 'too thin' and then a few months later as 'too fat'. A BBC survey[3] revealed that more than half of 12–16-year-old girls felt that their body image either stopped them from getting a boyfriend, or held them back from relaxing in a relationship. It can be helpful for girls to know that boys suffer a similar range of anxieties as they progress through adolescence; male celebrities present near-impossible, highly toned torsos as the perfect male body.

For support, it is important to focus on other attributes that are equally important when girls interact both with their peers and with adults. Finding a range of strong role models will also help girls to develop high self-esteem. One way to do this is to encourage girls to think of successful women in areas where they themselves have interests and talents. One teacher cited asking the girls in her school who their role models were, and overwhelmingly the majority cited their mothers as key inspirational figures in their lives. This is even more reason to ensure that girls have the self-confidence to keep media pressure in perspective now before they themselves become mothers.

Those who cited role models other than their mothers listed a range of women from different areas:

- *'Anne Frank for holding on to her optimism and faith'.*
- *'Jane Tomlinson who, despite being diagnosed with terminal cancer, participated in a series of athletic challenges; she did the London Marathon three times, the London Triathlon twice, the New York Marathon once, and she cycled across the USA and Europe. She raised £1.85 million for charity. She is proof that you can achieve anything you want and nothing is impossible, even if you have huge obstacles in your way.'*

---

3 BBC Radio 1 *Newsbeat* and BBC Radio 1Xtra TXU, Feb 2007.

- *'I heard Shirin Ebadi, the 2003 Nobel Peace Laureate, speak last year at the PeaceJam youth weekend and she is a truly inspirational woman. I greatly admire her determination to convey the importance of women's rights in Iran, despite facing opposition from the Iranian government. She is able to persevere in this struggle, despite facing threats (including the removal of her Nobel Prize medal) and constant arrests. She has overcome the fear that many human rights activists face in Iran and her courage is astounding. She is a Muslim and I admire the influence this has had on her life because she is not afraid to stand up for what she believes in.'*
- *'Emma Thompson, as she has managed to combine both acting and writing in her life and is highly acclaimed for both.'*

Giving girls a sense of their own purpose and worth will go a long way towards helping them develop their own sense of identity and the confidence to be comfortable in their own skin.

School refusers — another duvet day

School refusal, or phobia, is sometimes confused with truancy. However, the former is not a situation in which the child 'bunks off' school to go shopping or hang about the town centre. Imagine a child who simply refuses to get out of bed. Imagine the frustration and bewilderment felt by the parent. And, most of all, imagine the overwhelming feelings that have led to one's child taking such a dramatic step. Here is one family's experience:

'Our daughter had a very difficult school trip, aged 13, and this seemed to be the tipping point when she stopped attending school regularly – and then refused to attend at all. For our daughter was a "school refuser".

'At about this time, my daughter was encouraged to keep a diary, which she chose to do in pictorial form. When I saw it, I was appalled. Appalled and frightened. The pages were black. Words such as "I hate myself" and "There's no point in living" leapt out at me. I needed help. We all needed help. And we were not getting it. I took the book to a senior social worker. It was clear she did not understand the problems we were facing. "She has got you round her little finger", she said. But others, including our doctor, did understand.

'Various coping mechanisms were attempted or explored – threats of penalties, rewards, advice on outcomes, etc. Deadlines came and went, punishments were implemented. Nothing seemed to improve the situation. Meetings were held with the school. Special provisions were offered and put in place: first in line for meals; come in late; leave early; private room for study; and more.

'It was after one of these meetings that I met one of the Deputy Head Teachers outside the school, and he confided that his brother had been a school refuser. Later, I was to meet a chief executive of a children's charity, and discovered that her niece had a similar problem. "school phobia" or "school refusal" seemed to be a bigger problem than I had imagined, but little was being done about it. Where were we to get help?

'It became clear that our child's needs were not being met by the local secondary school's support systems. While they did care and did try, this was just too big for them. We tried the local health service. Our doctors are excellent. The nursing staff is first class – but all seemed unable to help.

'While almost all of the support agencies did try to find a solution, nothing seemed to make a difference. We felt pushed and pulled by conflicting demands, not helped, it must be said, by our daughter, who would often be uncommunicative or even walk out of these consultations. She found it frustrating, with the continued promises of help to bring an end to her problems that never seemed

95

*to work for her and left her feeling very negative about accepting
help – or seeing another professional.'*

A child is affected in many ways by not attending school. There
might be a loss of self-esteem, a sense of general anxiety, an
inability to travel on public transport or separate from the parents
and a slowing in personal development.

Typical refusers may also be sensitive to the point of timidity,
being unduly wounded by adverse comments from teachers, and
have unrealistically high goals for themselves; they may then
become excessively upset at their perceived failures.

*'Throughout all of this, we had worked on the theory that if our
daughter were to get back into school, she would only be able to
do so if she maintained relationships with her friends. And they
did try. However, as the friends dwindled, links with the local school
became more tenuous.*

*'We were aware of an independent girls' school a little over an
hour away. We had tried schools nearer our home, both day and
boarding, but they seemed unwilling to provide the support
required. We attended a couple of meetings at the school to discuss
options and were impressed by the flexibility that the school was
prepared to offer and learnt of other girls who had similar difficulties. After almost a year out of school, we were pleased when
our daughter made a quick decision that she wanted to try this
school. Initially, it was just day to day – and by no means every
day. Later, she managed on overnight stay, and slowly we built
up to full boarding. But even then, some days were taken as "duvet
days". Regular communication with school staff, and encouraging
texts and emails on days she stayed at home, helped maintain
the links.*

*'I am in no doubt that this school's adaptable and very supportive
approach will be the turning point on which our daughter's future*

hinges. University is still some way off, as is independent living, perhaps. But we are making steady progress.'

We are not good at sharing our anxieties about our children. We are prepared to extol their virtues – but not to publicise their failings. As a result, it is difficult to identify options that may help us, as parents, to cope and to find solutions. www.school refuser.org.uk is a site that offers support for parents of school refusers. Its aim is to demonstrate that parents are not alone in facing this situation and that support is available.

Thoughts from a Head – girls in pink?

The discussion has raged for decades, with varying degrees of concern. It was a major issue in the Seventies – should girls be brought up as girly girls in pink and skirts and have doll-centred toys, or did this just perpetuate the (domestic, and lower) position of women in society?

There was less plastic then, of course, so although little girls' clothes might be pink, at least the wheelbarrows were not. Some girls were hardly allowed more than a teddy bear to cuddle, and were raised almost entirely on toy cars and Meccano.

In recent years, as disposable incomes have risen, children have had more things. Manufacturers have realised that if everyone associates girls with pink, everything is available in pink and every little girl associates her identity with pink, parents and others will buy everything in pink for a girl – even if a family already owns said items in blue for an older boy. Gardening sets are in pink or blue, wellington boots are pink with hearts or blue with football designs, and pink fairies and princesses are everywhere.

Does it matter? Probably not, if parents understand what is happening and go no further down the pink path than they wish to – or can afford to. The best way for children to make the most of the advantages of their gender is to have strong and appropriate role models, who are themselves comfortable within themselves as well as within their gender role. But the concern is valid if girls are not encouraged to play in ways that develop those parts of their brain leading to an interest in numbers and maths, logic and science, and their application in technology and engineering. Eventually, most girls lose interest in pink, as the desired colour palette broadens, but it can be a real loss if by then they think only boys play football or understand basic engineering.

So parental expectation that all children, regardless of their gender, should be encouraged to play with all sorts of things and do every kind of activity make it more likely that girls are able to develop their science-side. Just as their brothers might learn when very young how to be caring, sharing dads in the future if they have characters of some kind to play with and care for.

So if your household has succumbed to girliness, just check that the pink princess has a toolset stored with her tiara so she can mend it when it suffers from too much wear, and that she could construct a tower as well as hang her sparkling, braided hair down from it, when thinking of ensnaring a passing prince.

Self-esteem Q&A

My daughter has become painfully shy

Q: My 14-year-old daughter has a small group of friends at school, which seems to work well most of the time. However, my daughter is painfully shy and will not get involved in school clubs or in any activities outside school. This is to such a degree that she refuses to go to town with her peers and has stopped inviting them to sleepovers at our house, although she would happily do this up to age 12. This term she has been to two sleepovers with one of the other girls at her house but refuses to invite her to ours. She says she finds it difficult to hold conversations and is often left out by the others. More recently, the others have been talking about going to the cinema with a group of boys and have not asked my daughter to join in. I know the other girls are very socially active and some already have boyfriends. My daughter is a very young 14-year-old and would be horrified to have to speak to boys at the moment.

I have tried to explain that it is quite normal to feel awkward in some social situations and maybe she should just ask the girls if she could come to the cinema, too. I have suggested she ask her group of friends, or even some other girls, to the cinema, etc., or have a sleepover, but she says she cannot do that as she feels so inadequate. I really worry about her, as even as a family, we cannot prise her out of the house at weekends to go clothes shopping, etc. I have written to her school and spoken to the Pastoral Head, but nothing positive seems to have come of it. Any suggestions?

A: Your daughter's situation at school is not unusual. At the moment, it would be best to focus on her happiness during the school day and to make sure that she has somewhere to go where she feels comfortable at breaks and lunchtimes. Ask her how she spends her time and what happens with her small group of friends. Please ask the school to give ideas about this and to check that your daughter is okay at these times. Ask to speak to your daughter's form tutor or Head of Year.

Sleepovers are very difficult social occasions, even for less shy girls, and not the best way to help friendships. She is clearly uncomfortable with bringing people home at the moment, as she would feel responsible for hosting the sleep-over, so I would not push this. If you know the mothers of one or two of her closest friends, you might be able to quietly ask for their help in arranging a less threatening social event. If she is not keen on clothes shopping, perhaps you could go on a shopping trip for yourself and then happen to visit some of the shops for her age group to bring her back something she might like.

She will mature over the next couple of years and hopefully things will become easier for her in mixed company. To increase her confidence, perhaps you could encourage her to take part in some activities outside the school with other young people, such as church groups, camps, sports activities or helping in the community. If she could be persuaded to go on a residential school trip during the holidays, this might also help. If you feel that her self-esteem is very low indeed and she might need some professional help, ask the school if they have an independent listener or trained counsellor who could help your daughter. Seek out the help of relatives who are close to her to find someone that she would confide in. Above all, keep talking to her and make sure her time at home is happy and without pressure.

Q: Why does my daughter's self-esteem matter so much?

A: Your daughter's self-esteem will determine much of what she says and does and how she reacts throughout her teenage years. For most girls, self-confidence is slowly acquired, hard won and easily bruised. Generally, girls are more open in displaying their vulnerability, more needy of affirmation and praise, and strive far harder to please. Once they hit their teenage years, it all gets far more complex and you enter the minefield of apparently totally irrational, emotional responses.

Q: Why does my daughter react so badly to criticism?

A: Girls, more than boys, depend more upon the approval of others, are more likely to modify their behaviour to win approval, to accept a low valuation of themselves and to automatically assume they are somehow wrong. Many girls cannot cope with criticism of any sort. An innocuous comment can be devastating and result in hours of misery-inducing self-analysis, as she struggles to work out why it was said and what it means to her. As a parent, the situation is further complicated by the very nature of the relationship, and there will be days when this really matters and others when it will count for nothing.

Q: My daughter gets really upset if the teachers criticise her. Why is this?

A: The role of teachers will sometimes be a benefit because they are outside the family and their opinion or advice might be regarded differently. But there will also be pitfalls for teachers. Pointing out a simple error in subtraction will convince your daughter that her teacher believes her to be 'rubbish at maths'. Even compliments can have a negative effect: if a teacher comments on how nice she looks today, she may wonder why they didn't say that yesterday.

Q: Why does she get embarrassed so easily?

A: One of the greatest fears of any girl is that of being 'shown up'. This will include anything at all that puts her in the spotlight. At times, such moments will make no sense to you whatsoever. Examples can range from the trivial to the major: telling a friend what your daughter did recently while in your daughter's earshot; her father dancing in public or telling her friends jokes; commenting on an outfit she is trying on in a shop; being invited on to the stage to be presented with an award at school or having something she has achieved read out in assembly; having to answer questions in class or perform in a concert. What each instance has in common is the potential for embarrassment and that, in itself, is enough.

Letting Go

From her first day at school to the day she sets up her own home, raising your daughter presents you with a continuous stream of challenges. It is for you to educate and advise her, to consider the pros and cons and then to find the courage to let her go. Whether it's her first sleepover or shopping trip with friends, sending her off to senior school, boarding school, university or on a 'gap year' – each causes a concerned parent deeply-felt anxieties. Is she ready? Will she manage? Will she be safe and happy or lost and vulnerable? Enabling your daughter to take many small steps with confidence involves teaching her, encouraging her and then letting her go.

Letting go — off to boarding school

Most likely, this will have been the biggest decision you have made for your daughter so far – whether she is 7, 11 or 16. It may be that this is a family tradition or you are a first-time boarding parent. You can prepare your daughter, whatever her age, for the separation of weekdays or term time away from home. Ideally, make sure that she is used to staying away from you for short periods with friends or grandparents from an early age. Be enthusiastic yourself about the fun and opportunities she will have at boarding school. Make sure that she has the correct uniform and kit; fitting in will be a major worry for her. Take advantage of any offer by the school for trial weekends or nights in the boarding house. Choose her school carefully and, if possible, make sure that your daughter has felt involved in the decision.

It is normal for your daughter to feel homesick when she first goes away and it is normal for you to feel separation anxiety. Remember when you first took her to nursery or pre-school, and you both cried? Remember how quickly she settled into the routine. Most children do not cry all day or night and soon become involved in the situation in which they find themselves and make friends. At school, lessons will occupy the day, then there will be after-school activities, and it is usually only at bedtime that your daughter will feel homesick. Take the advice of the houseparents; they will be hugely experienced in dealing with homesickness, as well as any other problems.

All teenage girls face friendship issues, regardless of which school they attend: wanting a best friend, falling out and hurting each other in the way they do best – verbally. As girls get older, they will grow out of it and it is part of growing up and developing their own ability to cope with any difficulties. For you as a parent, it can be devastating at the time, since your first and only instinct is to defend and protect your daughter. You will know when it is more than the normal quarrels between teenage girls, where they fall out with their best friend one day and are best friends again two days later. If it is more than that, do not hesitate to contact the school and ask them to intervene. Girls can rarely sort out these issues for themselves when they become extreme and need a sympathetic, but emotionally uninvolved, adult to help them. In the end, it is a valuable life lesson that you do not like or get on with everyone, but you learn to be able to work alongside people who will never be your best friend. At school your daughter will always have someone she can go and talk to. Many schools ask the older girls to keep an eye on the younger ones and to provide a sympathetic ear and friendly face. If your daughter appears to be unhappy, it will not go unnoticed. As a parent, you have an equal obligation to keep the school informed if your daughter is upset by anything happening at home. It is in everyone's interest that your daughter is happy and settled at school and is getting the best from her boarding experience.

Remember why you chose boarding school for your daughter. It is great fun and she will develop the ability to mix with a wide range of people. She will develop independence, good work habits and the ability to live reasonably tidily in a small space. She will have lots of opportunities and will have friends for life.

Letting go – gap years and university

It will seem like no time at all since you held that baby girl in your arms, took her for her first day at school, supported her through GCSEs, AS levels and A levels and suddenly the end is in sight. That little girl is about to fly the nest, move on her own into the adult world and step out of your protection and control. She thinks she is completely grown-up and is excited about the next move. Her confidence will be high. Although she may have some moments of doubt and fear of the unknown, she will be unlikely to admit them openly until the time to leave gets close, if at all. Try to remember how you felt at the same stage in your own life.

The best way you can help your daughter is to be excited for her and her new adventure and next phase of her life. Wherever she is going, she will be changed by the experience and will grow up while she is away. The person who returns will still be your daughter, but she will have had to make choices and decisions for herself, found new friends, lived on her own, had her own experiences – some of which you would not wish to know about and, if you do know, would rather she hadn't had.

There is a lot you can do in advance to prepare her for this big move. Discuss with her the issues of drugs, alcohol, contraception and keeping safe. Rehearse situations with her: 'What would you do if . . . ?' Try to let these conversations arise naturally in the months before she leaves (easier said than done), or your daughter will immediately switch off and dismiss your concerns airily. The night before departure is not the time to go through all these things: that night she will need all your confidence in her ability to cope; you should have been preparing her for months before. There is, however, a fine line between sensible preparation and sapping her self-confidence or projecting your own worst fears on to her. Your own worst fears are unlikely to materialise; fortunately, rape and murder are still rare and, with modern technology, the world has become a smaller place. If your daughter is going off to university, remember that she is now a young adult; her university will not communicate with you if she is falling behind with her work, is in deep debt or doing brilliantly – this will now be up to her.

Most people make friends quickly when they go away, even if those friends do not last beyond the first term of university or to the next stop-off in gap-year travel, but there is safety in numbers. Universities now hold briefing sessions for new students, telling them where it is not safe to wander and many also run late-night buses for students. Talk to your daughter about going out in a group and taking it in turns for one person to stay sober to keep an eye on the rest and to make sure everyone sticks together and gets back safely. Tell her to always trust her instincts. If she feels uneasy or uncomfortable, she is always best getting herself out of the situation.

If your daughter is going on a gap-year adventure, look at the Foreign Office website and read as much you can with her about the countries she will be visiting. Make sure she has any injections required and that she takes advice on equipment such as rucksacks and the safest way to carry money, as well as any cultural differences she needs to be aware of. Make sure you can get money to her quickly in an emergency and encourage her to keep a blog and use email to keep in touch with you. The blog will provide a wonderful memory for her on her return and will also reassure you while she is away.

Once she has gone, there will be a huge void in your life, particularly if she is the last child to leave home. Teenage girls are wonderful company, even when they are asserting their independence, being stroppy, playing their music at full blast or arguing about what time they have to be in at night. Many girls talk constantly, and you will miss her presence terribly when she first leaves. You will miss her constant chatter. It will be like bereavement, as you miss her presence in the house. You need to plan for this and move on to the next stage of your own life, as she may never again live full time at home. Her father may have more fears about her safety than about anything else, as he will feel unable to protect her from the unsuitable men she is bound to meet and he will remember himself at that age. Remember, there are advantages for you, too: you have your freedom and do not have to consider her at every moment. She has been launched into the world and has her own life to lead, her own decisions to make. She is a young adult. Your job is done.

Rites of passage — piercings and tattoos?

Beautification rituals, whether piercings, tattoos or make-up, have been part and parcel of girls' lives from a young age for years. Whether ear piercing is done at a high-end boutique shop or with a needle and a box of matches in the school loos, girls are eager to engage in the rites of passage seen as adulthood.

Today, ear piercing is common and facial and body piercings have become familiar. Celebrity role models sport a wide range of tattoos, and there is much discussion of body modification too private to display. Associations between decorative individuality and rebellion make it unsurprising that many teenage girls form strong views and are keen to experiment.

As we encourage our daughters to become independent thinkers, objecting to piercings and tattoos on the grounds of our own personal preference is unlikely to hold much sway. A consultation with a group of sixth form girls showed common sense and a considerable consensus on basic issues:

- *'A girl's body is her own, but the piercing/tattoo thing might be just a phase that I'll regret.'*
- *'Right now, we're "cool, independent teenagers". But walking down the aisle, you might want the option of a strapless dress without your ex-boyfriend's name scored across your back!'*
- *'Parents shouldn't forbid it. I was forbidden from getting certain bits of my ears pierced, so obviously I went and got them done as soon as I could at a festival (a really bad idea).'*

These girls agreed that piercings and tattoos should be treated differently, echoing the current legal restrictions. They viewed many types of piercings as acceptable. As a parent, you could set a reasonable period of time, perhaps six months, to test your daughter's resolve before she gets it done, but ultimately helping to ensure hygienic and safe treatment is essential. If things do go wrong, it is better that you know and are involved.

Concentrate on open discussion of facts – for example, that tattoos (and facial piercings) might deter potential employers, the way in which tattoos blur and spread with age, the scarring that can result from tattoo removal, the problems that lower back tattoos may cause for pregnant women who need epidurals, etc. Girls are usually aware that some forms of piercing have a high incidence of infection and can scar, but does your daughter know that a tongue stud may damage the enamel on her teeth or that infected ear cartilage piercings usually result in surgery as antibiotics will not work? There is some serious advice against 'corset' piercing; there are plenty of off-putting and gruesome images on the internet.

Do make sure that you are well informed before entering into debate with your daughter. There are many websites available; some you might prefer your daughter not to see, but which she may well have reviewed already. There are some web pages listed at the back of this book that are particularly informative.

If your daughter still wants a tattoo as she approaches 18, the website www.about.com/tattoos/bodypiercings is produced by an enthusiast. It is adult in its approach but absolutely clear about the health and safety issues involved; it might have more impact than obviously 'safe' NHS advice.

GROWING UP

Letting go Q&A

Is my daughter old enough to go out on her own?
Q: My daughter will be starting senior school in September, but she is already asking to go on solo shopping trips and other activities with her friends. I think she is still too young, but other parents are clearly allowing it. Am I being over-protective?

A: It can be difficult to know how to respond when your daughter asks you a seemingly straightforward question for the first time, such as 'Can I go to the cinema with my friends?' or 'Can I have a Facebook account?' In your opinion, it feels too soon, but you know that your daughter's friends are already doing these things. You do not want your daughter to be isolated because she can't join in with her friends, yet bowing to peer pressure on everything is not necessarily the best way forward.

Depending on the nature of the request, you may consider whether it is something you feel strongly about. If so, it is non-negotiable at the moment. It is helpful for you to know exactly why this is so that you can articulate these reasons to your daughter. Your daughter knows that she will have to accept your final decision on some things.

However, it can often be the case that she is quite relieved you have said no as she might not feel ready to do certain things, but peer pressure makes her feel that she should at least try!

However, there may be other issues on which you feel able to meet her halfway. For example, you might feel uncomfortable about your daughter going to see a film with her friends because of the location of the cinema, or because public transport is not easy. There may be a way to compromise so that your daughter feels that you are attempting to find a solution, as well as understanding why you are concerned. Establishing ground rules at home for the whole family, such as calling when arriving at a destination and giving an expected return time, will reassure you as to her whereabouts; she will do it automatically because it is what everyone in the family does all the time.

Parents often find that when their daughter starts senior school is one of the most difficult times to let go. Everything is very different for you, too; you do not see the class teacher at the beginning and end of the day and it can feel like you are sending your daughter into a 'black hole'. This is often compounded because you get very little feedback from your daughter as to how she feels things are going. Be reassured that this is normal and it is the start of your daughter seeking out more independence for herself as school becomes her world. Senior schools do try to find as many ways as possible to communicate with parents, so it may be helpful for you to find out your point of contact if you do have any questions.

Generally speaking, girls take this new-found independence in their stride. Having explored all the options and set out clear ground rules, it is up to us as parents and teachers to find the courage to let girls have a go and try things out for themselves.

Piercings – dealing with your daughter's requests

Q: How can I dissuade my daughter from having her ears stretched into those big loops. I think it is called tunnelling. She's 16 and just about to start in the sixth form and says it's her body, but I worry that her ears will be deformed for life. I know she is worried about her appearance and I don't want to stop her doing anything she feels will give her confidence — I've suggested other less intrusive piercings if she must — but she is dead set on having huge holes in her ears. Persuasion and argument haven't worked and I'm tempted to lay down the law and say she will have to move out if she has it done but then what if she does and ends up on the streets?

A: Many parents have had similar experiences. All too often our daughters disregard our advice and pleas, adamant that they know best, that they will always feel the way they do now and that we can't possibly understand. Here are a couple of suggestions: check whether parents' approval is needed for what sounds like a very invasive procedure for an under 18-year-old; try the tack of 'What will this look like when you're 40?' perhaps suggesting she imagines what you'd look like with the same piercings. It's wise to avoid making threats that you wouldn't want to carry out, such as asking her to move out. In the end, she's your daughter, you clearly love her and are communicating effectively even if she is maintaining her own position.

So many girls and young women lack confidence, particularly in their appearance. Peer groups and the media can make the most physically gorgeous girl feel inadequate despite parental reassurance. Perhaps you could offer her some shopping money to buy new clothes or accessories so she can start sixth form with a fresh wardrobe? Occasionally, bribery is an acceptable strategy! Many girls who get piercings and tattoos do come to regret it in later life, and no amount of 'I told you so' can ever undo it.

Am I indulging her every whim?

Q: My 13-year-old daughter always seems to be asking for more — trips and outings, new clothes, different clubs and activities, etc. She seems to want to try a new sport or musical instrument on a regular basis. I have tried to give her as many opportunities as I can, but it's costing a fortune with no real results or even satisfaction to show for it, and I'm starting to think that I'm just indulging her every whim. Where should I draw the line?

A: It sounds like you're trying to be a generous parent, but it does sound a bit as if you are in danger of holding on too much and overindulging her. As parents, we need to educate our daughters about what is reasonable to ask for and what is not. Even if it may not feel like it, it is kind to say no sometimes and to explain why. As an adult, your daughter will not have an unlimited amount of money in her budget, either, so she needs to learn the value of money now. It is fair for you to set an allowance for clothes each month and to encourage her to keep within that allowance. It is fair for you to decide how many outings and trips she is allowed and then to say no to the others. (It is not possible for many families to afford a lot of the expensive school trips on offer.)

Most children stick with one or two musical instruments and do not keep changing. If you are paying for lessons, it is reasonable to suggest that she should stick with one instrument for at least two years before giving up and trying others. She needs to understand commitment to certain activities and skills so that she can get the best out of them and work through the inevitable difficulties of learning something new.

Perhaps work out how much of your household budget should go on your daughter and then assign amounts for the various types of expenditure. Discuss this with her and treat her more like an adult. Stick to what you decide, otherwise you will be back to square one!

It is okay to say no to your daughter. As the parent, you set the limits and that is quite right and appropriate.

GROWING UP

Bullying

Girls can be bullies. Girls can be victims. What can you do to prevent your daughter from being either? How can you encourage her to stand up for herself and others?

Girls and bullying

Recent research from the universities of Warwick and Hertfordshire identifies differences between girls' and boys' bullying.

One of the findings showed that girls are more likely to be the victims of sustained bullying than boys. Such assertions add fuel to the misleading assumption that girls are more malicious and cruel than boys. Based on extensive experience of girls' and boys' schools, and decades of experience as both Heads and Deputy Heads, we hope to offer a useful overview of girls' bullying behaviour, and their response to the bullying behaviour of others.

First of all, girls are not naturally more malicious and cruel than boys, just as women are not more malicious and cruel than men. However, girls are both more subtle and more sensitive. Girls are also more likely to interpret unfriendly behaviour as bullying.

In fact, we all tend to use the word 'bullying' too readily these days. Children will occasionally be unkind to each other. Friendships shift and, when they do, some children can feel left out and hurt. But 'bullying' presupposes a sustained period of deliberately inflicting pain in some way. Relationships tend to matter very much to girls. Being accepted and being popular are particularly important to them, and they are more sensitive and easily hurt when they feel isolated.

Bullying appears to take place in every school (and probably most work environments, too). However, schools have become far more adept at anticipating and preventing bullying, spotting and dealing with problems if they do arise. They will have policies in place to guide them and make expectations clear to the children. They will openly state that bullying is not tolerated in their communities. And they will discipline bullies and support those who are the target of bullying on a case-by-case basis.

Schools also work to support and build the confidence of those who are the targets of bullying. Given that we can all find ourselves on the receiving end of some sort of intimidation, we need to develop the strategies to defend and assert ourselves, and schools can help to give your daughter the tools to deal with such situations.

If you feel your daughter is being bullied, talk to the staff at her school and work with them to help her. You may have to work hard to persuade your child that talking to the school is the right way forward, but, in our combined experience, it is.

Coping with girls' bullying

The way in which girls bully is very different from the way in which boys bully. Girls tend to worry far more about relationships than boys do and it is important not to be dismissive of this. Encourage your daughter to keep things in perspective and not to overreact to everything that happens within her friendship group, but appreciate that she can feel truly miserable by the group dynamics within her social circle.

You can help her by:

- listening to her concerns
- helping her to develop the strategies to cope with them. She must develop strategies for herself – you can't sort out such problems for her. As she grows up, she will need the skills to deal with relationships of all kinds, some of them confrontational and threatening
- encourage her to talk to you about what is happening and how she is feeling. If the problems involve groups at school,

GROWING UP

persuade her that you need to talk to the school staff about the issue so that they are aware and can work with you to support her

Girls will include or exclude each other, depending on friendship fluctuations and loyalties. Technology gives them new ways of doing this – texts, email, instant messages, internet chatrooms and websites offer perfect opportunities for manipulative girls to talk to and about each other and to inflict pain in increasingly imaginative ways. Banning and policing are not the answer; encouraging responsible and discriminating use of technology is.

We need to listen to and help to educate our children rather than simply hoping to protect them and cushion them from the realities of human interaction. It is important that you help your daughter realise:

- you cannot make people be friends with you
- friendships are two-way
- friendships must be worked at in order to thrive

Having said that, your daughter should never have to accept being made unhappy, isolated or frightened.

So it's all about communication – with your daughter, with her friends and with the school if the social group in question is a school group. Hard though it is, in some situations girls need to be persuaded to move away from social groupings that are negative and unhealthy and instead to find a new friendship group, in which individuals treat each other more kindly.

If your daughter feels friendless, encourage her to reach out to someone else she thinks may also be lonely. Suggest she tries the line, 'Would you like to come to lunch with me?', rather than always asking, 'Can I come to lunch with you?'

What do I do if I find out that my daughter is a bully?

It takes real courage to face up to the fact that despite everything you have done to bring up your daughter to be kind and caring to others, it has emerged that she is demonstrating unkind or harmful behaviour towards others. Usually, it is the school that will bring this to your attention, and although they will try to do so sensitively, you may experience a whole range of emotions: shame, anger, denial . . . but what is most important is that you put all of these emotions to one side. Your daughter needs your help, and you will need all your emotional resources to help to support her.

It is almost certainly the case that the situation your daughter finds herself in is a messy one. Rarely is it the case that bullying comes from nowhere – very often, a bully has herself been bullied, and this may not have been picked up at school, or will only emerge as you get to the bottom of what is going on. Avoid trying to apportion blame, however, and focus instead on what you can do to help to change your daughter's behaviour. Your daughter's school would not have broached such a sensitive subject with you if they did not have some concrete evidence, and you need to accept this if you are going to work together to help her to reorientate herself.

Ultimately, both you and your daughter's school want her to be happy, and it can almost be guaranteed that if your daughter is bullying others, she is unhappy to some degree. If you are looking for some reassurance, this should help – your daughter is not a fundamentally bad person, and her behaviour to others is at least in part a reflection of her unhappiness. It is possible to help her, and you need to work with her school to do this consistently and calmly.

There are three main strategies to consider in your approach: counselling, boundary-setting and relationship-building. Your first priority should be to arrange a counsellor for your daughter

– see if her school can help to recommend someone. Your daughter really needs to see a counsellor as soon as possible to help her unravel why she is behaving in this way, and to help her behave differently. This is unlikely to be a quick fix, but it is essential for her future wellbeing. Don't be surprised or feel you are a failure if the counsellor suggests involving the whole family in this counselling – just see it as another way to help your daughter.

The school – and you – will want to set firm boundaries for your daughter's behaviour; again, work with the school so that you are all following the same principles. Your daughter must stop bullying, and if this means that she is not allowed in certain places at set times for a while, then go along with this. Together, you and the school will be giving your daughter the best chance to help her change what she is doing.

Remain closely in touch with your daughter's school, and once things have begun improving, be guided by them to help your daughter mend bridges and rebuild relationships. Ultimately, everyone needs to forgive and move on, but this will take time and a lot of effort. Don't expect it all to happen overnight – but if you actively seek to make a difference in your daughter's behaviour, and you work with as many professionals as you can, it will happen.

Bullying — helping children to understand

Ask a group of teachers what is the most important ingredient of a school, and they will probably say good teaching. Ask parents and they may also say good teaching, plus good exam results, good facilities and good pastoral care. Ask pupils the most important ingredient, and they may say 'no bullying'. This should not be a surprise. However much you enjoy learning, if you don't feel safe, school will be an ordeal. Imagine how dreadful it must be to wake up every day and face the torment of victimisation in whatever form it may take, whether physical or psychological aggression, exclusion or ridicule.

Bullying can be hard to deal with, partly because it usually happens when adults are not present. That doesn't mean that you do not try to tackle it when it does occur. A school that dismisses unhappiness, stating that bullying is just a normal part of growing up, is a cynical place worth avoiding. However, bullying is difficult to tackle because children, and girls in particular, can be fickle and changeable in their attitudes, largely because of their own internal uncertainties about their evolving identity. Girls at this stage can be like dodgems at a fairground; little cars careering in different directions, colliding one moment, coming alongside the next. Employing a range of tactics, a child can mount a sustained campaign to isolate someone and then suddenly be sweet and inclusive, only to resume the unkindness once again.

There are books and websites galore offering advice on how to deal with bullying, but one of the best descriptions of this is to be found in the novel *Cat's Eye* by Margaret Atwood. The narrator has two friends, Grace and Carol. A third girl, Cordelia, moves into the area and the torment begins:

I'm standing outside the closed door of Cordelia's room. Cordelia, Grace and Carol are inside. They're having a meeting. The meeting is about me. I am just not measuring up, although they are giving me every chance. I will have to do better. But better at what? I lean against the wall. From behind the door comes the indistinct murmur of voices, of laughter, exclusive and luxurious.

Carol is in my classroom, and it's her job to report to Cordelia what I do and say all day. They're there at recess and at lunchtime. They comment on the kind of lunch I have, how I hold my sandwich, how I chew. On the way home I

119

have to walk in front of them, or behind. In front is worse because they talk about how I'm walking, how I look from behind. 'Don't hunch over,' says Cordelia. 'Don't move your arms like that.' They don't say any of the things they say to me in front of others, even other children: whatever is going on is going on in secret, among the four of us only. Secrecy is important, I know that: to violate it would be the greatest, the irreparable sin. If I tell I will be cast out for ever.

Cordelia doesn't do these things or have this power because she's my enemy. Cordelia is my friend.

She likes me, she wants to help me, they all do.

Understanding behaviour doesn't mean condoning it. Children need to see bullying outlawed at school to prevent them turning into bullying adults. Bullying in the workplace is now a recognised problem. Combating bullying is also an important issue for adults.

Thoughts from a Head — the scourge of cyber-bullying

Holly, who was a pupil at another school in my hometown, took her own life. It seems that she was the subject of cyber-bullying. Judging by all the tributes paid, this was a normal young girl who was loved and had everything to live for. Anything other than expressing heartfelt condolences to her family in their devastation and to all those at her school coping with grief would be intrusive speculation, so instead, let me turn to the question of how to influence behaviour so that we can seek to guide our offspring safely through these often turbulent teenage years.

We live in an age of regulation and guidance: how to keep fit; how to avoid obesity; how to protect children from abuse by vetting everyone who has contact with them; how much drink is harmful; how to recycle your waste, etc.

And yet, all the regulation and medical advice do not stop the growing problems of alcohol consumption and obesity. All the stringent health and safety advice now in existence did not stop an E. coli outbreak when a farm did not act responsibly. If we let common sense prevail and did everything we were told was good for us, how different the world would be. No more couch potatoes; no more inebriates throwing up on the pavements on a Saturday night; no more speeding fines; no more crime.

Schools are communities that have to have a set of policies and rules in order for everyone to live harmoniously together. The policies stem from the principles of what is deemed ethical and considerate behaviour. Producing the policies is the easy bit. Making them work is harder.

The same goes for parents trying to set some guidelines around a teenage daughter's budding social life. In this post-deferential age, just telling young people, especially girls, to do something: line up in silence; tie your hair back; complete your homework; be in by 11 pm; will work up to a point but is hard to sustain unless they see the justification for the instruction and believe that to comply is in their best interests.

This does not mean that young people are averse to authority; on the contrary, they welcome consistent teachers and parents who care enough to be firm but fair. But they expect, quite reasonably, to have the school's or parents' stance explained before they will buy into it.

Schools and parents have to take seriously their role to provide a good moral education and work relentlessly at setting an example and encouraging open communication and honest reflection.

Enter peer pressure, an overworked phrase at the best of times. The same quality that you rely on when influencing pupils to adhere to the school's expectations of behaviour, namely, the desire to belong, can also be exploited negatively, sometimes with devastating consequences.

Teenage children have a set of identities (daughter, student, future professional, school friend, girl friend, Facebook friend) and can compartmentalise the different settings in their lives with remarkable self-control and inscrutability, meaning that parents or teachers cannot always detect mounting problems in a part of a child's life from which they are excluded. To counteract this, school staff and parents have to work doubly hard to express affection and concern, to engage and to reiterate what they consider to be sensible.

These are not new phenomena any more than bullying is a new phenomenon, but the added dimension of the online community sites has certainly taken the need to belong and copy the behaviour of the pack on to a whole new level. Young people, even the most loved and balanced, have a lot to contend with these days.

Bullying Q&A

Q: My daughter is being bullied and her school isn't doing anything about it. Where do I go from here?

A: It's unclear from your question what steps you've already taken, but is it fair to assume you have spoken to the school staff about your concerns? If so, contact the school again, tell them the situation is still unresolved and ask to set up a meeting between relevant pastoral staff, you and your daughter. At that meeting, talk through what has happened and how your daughter is feeling, and discuss what steps both she and the school can take to help to address the issues and to move forward. The school should take responsibility for dealing with the individuals accused of bullying. You also need to recognise that your daughter needs to develop strategies for dealing with such situations (which may not be confined to the world of school — this is a skill set she will need for life) so that you help to build her resilience, too. If the perpetrators are other girls, see also the 'Girls and bullying' section in this book and perhaps track down some of the work of Val Besag on the internet, which you may find helpful.

Bullying in the classroom

Q: My daughter has just started Year 8. The students in her girls' secondary school classroom have all bonded securely and feel strong enough to start teasing the new (male) science teacher. They plan innocent pranks before every lesson (nobody answers questions, annoying noises are made during lessons, class explanations are systematically interrupted . . .). Most of the girls go along with the leading pack, fearful that they will be isolated if they oppose them. What do you suggest is the appropriate course of action for my daughter and for us as parents?

A: Contact your daughter's Head of Year or form tutor and tell them what is happening. It sounds as though these girls have found a chink in their science teacher's armour. He needs some support and advice from senior managers on how to deal with and improve this situation. If other girls are joining in because they're afraid of being isolated, then this is a case of bullying — these girls are bullying their teacher. Meanwhile, reassure your daughter that she was being very responsible when she told you of her concerns and tell her that she is brave not to collude with the bullies. It might be worth pointing out that their understanding and learning of science will be suffering. Hopefully, some of the other girls will also realise that their behaviour is unkind and will join with your daughter.

Why is she always 'left out' — is this bullying?

Q: My 10-year-old daughter frequently returns from school complaining that she doesn't have a friend or is being left out. What can I do to help her? Isn't this bullying?

A: 'Friendship' and the need for a 'best friend' will be the most important issue in your daughter's life at this moment in time and will continue to be so for some years to come. It can be heartbreaking for parents and is perhaps the most commonly perceived act of bullying.

Girls can meet many obstacles when forming or maintaining friendships in their daily lives at junior school. From 'seat-saving' at lunchtimes to games in the playground that are, quite mysteriously, 'only meant for two', it is so easy for girls to feel excluded. Being left out from 'private words', 'secret conversations' or from that 'popular' girl's party is hurtful for even the most robust 10-year-old. While junior schools adopt many successful strategies such as 'friendship stops' in play-grounds or appoint 'friendship monitors' from among the older girls, parents can also help a great deal by avoiding the organising of 'exclusive' parties for their daughters at such a vulnerable time. Wherever possible, parents should include the whole class at parties for infant-age children; parents can check with their daughter's teacher to ensure that friends are not omitted unknowingly from celebrations, outings and treats. Parents can also be proactive in ensuring that a wide circle of friends is regularly invited home to play at different times.

Girls put considerable demands on each other and relish a friend whom they can trust and will stand by them, a friend who will not 'take sides'. We therefore have to provide a safe and secure environment both at home and at school, in which girls can grow as confident, caring and trustworthy individuals who never feel the need to betray someone's trust or friendship. We have to do all we can to nurture their self-esteem and to build girls' confidence and resilience so that they are able to accept and understand that friendships can and do move on. As girls get older and their characters develop, friendships can become transient and the demands girls place on each other change. Young girls, in particular, need our help and guidance in learning how to 'let friends go' sensitively. We can help by encouraging young girls to maintain a broad circle of friends and to be open and welcoming to new friendships. This is particularly important as 10-year-old girls prepare to move on to senior school. While girls may appear excited about meeting new friends in a new environment, they are inevitably apprehensive about leaving or losing their existing friends. Girls can become highly possessive of their friendships and the exclusive 'best friend' should be discouraged at this time.

At this time it can be extremely useful to remind girls of this familiar proverb:

> 'Make new friends, but keep the old,
> one is silver, the other gold.'

And, most importantly, make sure they understand that the only way to have a good, loyal friend is to be one!

Personal and internet safety

The media is full of horror stories of children being harmed. Is our world really such a dangerous place? How can you keep your daughter safe? These events hit the headlines because they are so unusual, yet they can give valuable examples of what you and your daughter should be aware of. The dangers are different at different ages: deep water when small, dark alleys when older, and then there are internet chat rooms. You can't wrap your daughter in cotton wool to keep her safe. A parent's job is to teach her boundaries and to maintain good communication. From going to the shops alone to setting off on a gap year, your daughter needs your calm support, reassurance and guidance.

Personal safety

The current trend for 'helicopter parents' who hover over their child, micro-managing every aspect of their life, is a disadvantage to these children. You need to help your daughter to develop the skills she herself will need to cope in the outside world rather than overprotecting her. Getting the right balance between wrapping her in a cocoon of cotton wool and leaving her exposed to real threats is not as difficult as it sounds.

You will not be alone. Your daughter's school will also be preparing her to deal with potential dangers – for example, through 'stranger danger' courses, Personal, Social and Health Education lessons and lessons on internet safety.

Focus on developing her self-confidence so she learns to say no and to be assertive. This is equally important, whether she is offered drugs or pressured to have sex or asked by a stranger to go with him 'to look for his lost puppy'. Always ask her where she is going, with whom, and agree when she is to be home. Mobile phones make communication much easier, but try to avoid telling her to ring you on the hour, every hour!

Internet safety

Consider whether it is wise to let her have a computer in her bedroom. If she is too young to be left alone at home, she is probably too young to be using the internet's communication tools without supervision.

Stay involved in how she is using the computer, look at her and her friends' web pages on social networking sites and check the computer's history. You could remind her that the police say anything on the internet is public, that malicious gossip is a serious offence and that employers (and teachers) check out these sites.

Remind her to tell you or another adult if she feels uncomfortable or unhappy about anything she reads online. There are several helpful sites, some of which are listed at the back of this book, where you can get advice and instruction if your IT skills are less developed than hers (as is likely!). Above all, keep talking with her, about your concerns as well as about possible threats to her safety. Once she is in her mid-teens, peer pressure will be the greatest influence in her life so any lecturing from you could be counter-productive. She needs strategies for managing the risks that are an inevitable part of life so that she can become a confident, competent and successful adult and use the 'wings' you have given her to fly.

The pursuit of liberty vs. stranger danger

When yet another case of child abduction or child abuse or, the ultimate horror, of child murder hits the headlines, the blood of every parent in the land runs cold. It only takes a very small leap of imagination to put ourselves in the position of those parents: what could we/they have done to prevent these terrible acts? Surely the fundamental role of a parent is to keep their beloved child safe? If it happens to any child, it could happen to our child.

We tell our children not to talk to strangers, but we also raise them to be polite and helpful. Recently, a group of 11 year old girls spent a day learning about "stranger danger" with Surrey Police. They were attentive and correctly answered the questions about how to keep themselves safe. At the end of the session the girls were sent outside for a break; here they met a man who was holding an empty dog lead and collar. He seemed upset and told them his puppy had slipped its leash. Could they help him look for it? Of course, they trotted off with him into the bushes in search of his mythical pet.

The girls were shamefaced when the policeman who was playing the part of the nice man who'd lost his puppy pointed out how easily they had fallen for his trick, but would they behave any differently in a slightly different situation?

A 13-year-old girl travelling home from school on her usual train felt uncomfortable about a man who seemed to be watching her rather too closely. He then moved seats so as to have a clearer line of vision of her. He got off at the same station as she did and seemed to be following her. This sensible and brave girl approached a group of older girls and told them her fears. One of the girls took a photo of the man on her mobile, then called 999.

Of course, as parents and teachers, that's what we want to happen. Because while we don't want our children to be fearful, timid or mistrustful of every unknown adult, neither do we want them to be overconfident and lacking in awareness of possible dangers. We want them to be able to evaluate situations calmly, weigh up likely risks and take appropriate action. We know we can't wrap them in cotton wool; indeed, to do so would also be dangerous, for how can a child assess an unfamiliar situation if she has never been exposed to risk?

These headlines appal us because we can identify with the emotions of those affected. But we must not forget that one of the reasons we are so greatly affected is because these kinds of events are so very rare. Many more children are killed in traffic accidents every hour of every day, yet these events don't make headlines because they're all too common. Do we warn our children sufficiently of the traffic danger that is far more likely to impact them than we do of stranger danger?

What are parents supposed to do?
We all want our daughters to have the freedom to be brave and bold, to view the world as a place of potential and excitement and to expect other people to treat them kindly. We do not want them looking for danger in every situation, crippled by terror and viewing every adult as a possible threat.

Is this so very different from how we help our toddlers to grow? We stop them putting their fingers into electric sockets but we don't stop them from going upstairs – we teach them how to do it safely. Surely this strategy should extend throughout their upbringing? We put stabilisers on their first bike and expect a few falls. Swimming pools are fenced off and we teach our children to swim. We teach them their name and address when small; we give them a mobile when they are older.

If we take it as given that our job is to provide our girls with a nest and also with wings, then we have to prepare them to leave us. As you gradually let go, encouraging your daughter to move with confidence towards independence, you will need to negotiate with her. You know her best so will be able to judge the new situations you face – for instance, when you can trust her to go out with friends without an adult. Keep communicating, tell her when you're going to check up with other mothers and accept that some fights are inevitable but not terminal. Help her to grow those wings safely, confident that if you do, she will keep flying back to the nest, but on her own terms, and that you will be a successful parent.

Protecting and supervising your daughter on the internet

Protecting our children goes with the territory of being a parent. We warn and train them from a young age about the dangers of electricity, crossing the road and encountering strangers. When it comes to the internet, these principles still apply – even if we sometimes feel that we are not qualified to do so.

It is easy for us to install the 'Net Nanny' programme on our home PC and assume that that we have fulfilled our parenting responsibilities in this area. If we are to ensure that our children use the internet wisely and safely, we ourselves need to know our way around it. It is important that we talk about online experiences with our children. Just as with crossing the road, we cannot be there all the time, but it is worthwhile to spend some time going through the basics together. Young people often come across as highly competent on computers, but many have a blind spot when it comes to protecting their privacy, so don't be afraid to ask awkward questions.

Research has found that the more often 'significant adults' talk to young people about their experiences online (and occasionally monitor what they are doing), the less likely a young person is to engage in risky behaviour (defined as disclosing personal information, meeting up offline with someone they met online or sharing photos with strangers). The young people who did not have the adult intervention were four times more likely to agree to meet up with someone they met online.

As parents, we may have a level of control over the other people our children encounter in 'real space', but we cannot regulate whom our children meet in digital space. However, we can help them to make better decisions about their own safety when online. Some tips on supervising young teenagers:

- Keep the computer in a public place, preferably with the screen facing into the room, so that it can be seen when passing.
- Laptops with Wi-Fi mean that it is almost impossible for parents to have any handle on what their daughter is doing on the internet. Many parents consider that laptops are best suited to the older teenager.
- Beware that mobile phones with internet capability (which includes the majority of phones today) are likely to provide unfiltered access to the internet.
- Set clear rules for internet use.
- Insist that your children do not share personal information, such as their full name, address, phone numbers, full date of birth or passwords, with people they meet online.
- Don't just rely on 'Net Nanny'. As any school network manager will tell you, young people are experts at evading 'Net Nanny' programmes and pass information between themselves on how to do this. (This usually entails going to a site that is listed as safe, which then redirects the user to the desired, banned site.)
- The browsing history of a computer keeps a record of the sites that have been visited by a particular user. A deleted browsing history is likely to tell you as much as an undeleted one.
- Be aware that most internet browsers now allow for 'private browsing' sessions in which no browsing history is recorded.

• If your daughter types 'POS' when on a social networking site or on MSN, it means 'Parent Over Shoulder'. Draw your own conclusions!

Supervision of social networking sites

Your daughter is unlikely to want you as a 'friend' on a social networking site, but some parents make it a condition of being on Facebook when their children are starting out. It will give you the opportunity to keep an eye on your daughter's online friends. Parents with a social networking site profile are much better placed to help their daughter to protect her privacy. Parents need to keep up to date with how the privacy settings work (as these do change) and to talk these through with their daughter.

Useful links

For more on internet safety, see www.microsoft.com/protect/ parents/childsafety which outlines '10 things you can teach kids to improve their web safety' and also has some excellent age-related tips.

The website www.saferinternet.org also has some useful information on a range of internet safety issues.

For a guide to privacy on Facebook, try www.facebook.com/ privacy.

Social networking sites — the pros and cons

Social networking sites, such as Facebook and Bebo, can be great: keeping up with friends; making arrangements. But there can be downsides, too, and girls need to be aware of them and how to deal with situations that might arise.

Just as adults regret the impulsive email, for girls there is something about the immediacy of electronic communication that makes them drop their guard. That comment about what someone was wearing, which, if said face to face and with the appropriate 'softening' body language, might just have been okay, is there, with all the force of being in print, for all the world to see, and to add in their comments, with the inevitable resultant hurt and damage to friendships.

These situations are all the more difficult to untangle because contributors can make their comments under pseudonyms. For parents or schools, trying to establish the identity of 'Pretty Girl' is nigh on impossible – and, for girls, not knowing who's writing comments about you is often more hurtful than knowing who is!

So, how best to advise your daughter?

- If possible, especially with younger girls, place the computer in a family space so that you can keep a 'casual' eye on it. You'd be surprised how much use is made of social networking sites on computers in girls' rooms long after you think they're asleep!
- Set some guidelines around who your daughter gives access to her page and how long she can spend chatting to her friends.
- Discuss with her how to respond if messages start to get unpleasant.
- Remind her that what sounds clever and witty when spoken out loud may not be okay when seen on screen.
- Remind her that this kind of unpleasantness, especially if it goes on over a period of time or if a 'cyber gang' forms, is increasingly being considered by schools as bullying, with all the consequences that would arise if it were happening in school in 'real space'.

Understanding Facebook

For many parents and teachers, the world of Facebook is an alien place; it certainly operates under a different set of rules. The following is an attempt to unpack the two main dynamics of social networking sites.

Making 'friends'

When we as parents or teachers meet someone new, say at a drinks or dinner party, we trade snippets of personal information about ourselves as part of the 'friend-making process'. Where we work, where we went on holiday, our favourite film and what music we listen to – such is the stuff of social small talk. As we get to know someone better, the information we share about ourselves becomes more personal and, over time, the transition is made from casual acquaintance to friendship.

Friend-making is at the heart of sites like Facebook. But when young people 'make friends' on social networking sites, they operate in a totally different way – dinner party conventions do not apply here. The whole process is truncated into a millisecond, as they disclose their life story in a single mouse click, disgorging enormous amounts of personal information to relative strangers.

The dynamic in the world of social networking seems to be that the more information you give out, the more 'friends' you will have. Openness here is a virtue; a lack of disclosure is met with suspicion. Thus, there is a contractual basis to the way in which young people use social networking sites, as they trade personal information for popularity – this is a key driver behind such sites.

'Famous for . . .'

Social networking sites enable young people to emulate their role models, as we live in the age of celebrity. The famous live their lives in the eye of the media – the gossip pages of glossy magazines and fan websites share the most minute details of teenagers' role models. Reality TV shows such as *Big Brother* have fuelled this craze, with celebrities' most intimate moments broadcast to the world for public scrutiny.

So why should we surprised that young people want the same thing? Unprepared to wait for their fifteen minutes of fame, anyone is able to behave like celebrities and to put themselves permanently in the public eye, courtesy of Facebook. Young people are able to share their thoughts with their friends and to update the world on even the most banal aspects of their daily lives. For some, Facebook is their diary; for others, it is a vehicle for a 'second life': an opportunity to present themselves to the world as they would like to be seen.

Ultimately, Facebook harnesses the timeless need of young people to spend time together (their parents' generation did it on the phone) and satisfies a basic twenty-first century need to receive public recognition from one's peers.

When the virtual world meets the real world . . .

The following is an example of how the internet can catch people, and specifically young people, unaware.

A perfectly normal and very bright 14-year-old girl had taken a photo of an ex-best friend and, using some sophisticated software bought for her by her parents for an art project, combined the head of her ex-best friend with an indecent image she found online and then emailed it to all her friends. Next, the victim's mother came into the school office with the picture. The result: a double set of horrified parents and a girl mortified that the school had access to the picture.

Ironically, the week before this incident the school had hosted a strategy day, where the senior management team and staff had discussed several questions regarding the increasing use of information and communication technologies and the potential dangers. Despite the school's firewall, anti-virus software, anti-spyware, anti-malware and constant scrutiny of internet traffic within the school, plus the fact that survey results within the school indicated that 93% of staff felt they had warned pupils of the dangers, this bright, successful girl had succumbed to the most common misconception of the web: that what she did in the privacy of her own bedroom on the internet was between her and her friends. Unfortunately, she learnt the hard way that it isn't.

One of the key discussions at the staff meeting revolved around whether, despite having held a 'safety on the web' evening the previous year, the school needed to provide more advice for parents. While everything can be put in place within the school environment, technology is progressing so fast that even these safeguards can be skirted (for example, when pupils use their iPhones). The seemingly limitless online access some girls have at home also makes a nonsense of any school's measures.

Facebook, Bebo, chain emails, myface, Addys, buddy lists, Google Wave and similar software create an environment that can be more dangerous than crossing a road. None of us would allow a child to cross a road alone until we were convinced that they had learnt to navigate the process sufficiently, which is why it is so important to have rules in place to protect our digitally sophisticated, but still naive, children from dangers they may not yet foresee or understand.

Mobile phones — when, where and how much?

When is the right time for my daughter to have a mobile phone?
Mobile phones play a key role in ensuring pupil safety travelling to and from school. Girls need phones to be able to communicate with parents to arrange pick-ups or to keep them informed of when the buses and trains are running late. They afford a degree of protection to the lone traveller, and thus give reassurance to parents. Once your daughter is involved in after-school clubs, particularly ones that involve pick-ups after it has got dark, it makes sense for her to have a cheap, basic phone for emergencies.

There is no doubt that parents come under considerable pressure from their daughters, who argue, in time-honoured fashion, that 'everyone else has got one'. As with other areas, such as parties, curfews and alcohol, parents need to establish good lines of communication with other parents, so that they are not all played off against each other.

What about 3G mobile phones, or smart phones, with internet capability?
The problem with phones that have internet connectivity is that girls immediately have unrestricted internet access. On the positive side, this will enable them to look up useful information and to support their learning. However, it also means that they will be able to get on to social networking sites, such as Facebook.

Mobile devices with internet capability (either through dialling up or through Wi-Fi) are here to stay – indeed, they are becoming ubiquitous. We will not be able to restrict what our daughters are doing with them, so we need to ensure that they are cyber-safe and educated on how to use them wisely. Parents need to consider whether their daughter has sufficient maturity to make positive use of a phone with internet capability, while avoiding the inherent dangers and temptations.

How can I control how much my daughter uses her mobile?

Girls love chatting – they always have. Many of us who are now parents sat for hours on the family phone chatting to our friends. Today, young people just have more ways to chat: talking face to face; texting; on their mobiles; instant messaging; on Facebook and so on. The most significant difference is that, rather than chatting on the landline in the relatively public place at the bottom of the stairs, it is all much more private – away from parental eyes and ears. What is interesting is that young people now communicate much more by the written word than ever before.

The best way for parents to retain a degree of control over their daughter's use of their mobile phone is to limit the amount of credit that she has on her phone. A package that has an unlimited number of texts may appear attractive from a financial perspective, but it does give a green light to your daughter to spend an enormous amount of time texting.

Pay-as-you-go contracts are best for young teens. Ultimately, they give you greater control over your daughter's phone use. If the phone is in your name and you top up with small amounts, you can monitor how much your daughter is using the phone and you can also have regular conversations about her phone use.

Should mobile phones be allowed in schools?

Mobile phones clearly can be a distraction during lessons (texting under the desk, etc.), but they can also be of great use (pupils taking photographs of the board or of an experiment, for example).

Short of putting silver foil over all the windows, it is impossible to stop girls using phones in schools. They need to learn what is and what is not appropriate use. Most schools have an acceptable use policy to outline the school's stance on this matter.

Personal & internet safety Q&A

Q: How can I protect my daughter from paedophiles?

A: The actual risk is very small, but there are things you can do: remind her never to talk to, let alone accept sweets or a lift from, anyone she doesn't know, whether a man or a woman. Tell her that if you have to ask someone unknown to her to collect her, you will give them something of yours that she will recognise as proof that you sent them. Remind her that people on the internet are not always who they pretend to be. She should never give her real or full name or any details that could lead to an online 'friend' identifying or contacting her. But reassure her that the overwhelming majority of people are trustworthy and kind.

Personal development

At every stage in her life your daughter will be learning, experimenting and absorbing. She will need your help to develop strategies so she can negotiate the potential pitfalls, deal with disappointments and make good choices.

Growing up — a journey

From the moment she is born, your daughter is on a journey of discovery – learning first to think, walk, speak and do. Later in life, her discovery becomes more complex, as she asks: who am I, really? What is important to me? What do I want to do with my life? She learns how to make good choices, live a good life and be the person she is meant to be: this is her journey of self-discovery.

Self-discovery means learning who she is deep down and why, what matters to her in life and how she can determine the course of her life to ensure that she fulfils her potential, leading to a happy and satisfying existence. The more she knows about and understands herself, the greater the opportunities she will have to find happiness and contentment, and the more rewarding she will find her life.

Above all, you probably wish for your daughter to have an amazing and fulfilling life journey, which raises the following key questions as a parent:

What can you do to make sure that she makes the most of her travels?
How can you help her along the way? From the moment your daughter is born, she is learning who she is, and is beginning to carve out a path for herself. You have created her as a unique person who will have a unique journey, and the choices she

makes on the way will help to determine the direction and nature of this journey.

How does she learn how to make good choices?

Above all, your daughter will learn from her experiences. She will learn by what she sees, does and tries out. She will learn what she likes doing and what she doesn't. She will learn from her successes and she will learn from her failures. You can help to create opportunities for experiences – for success and for failure, for risk-taking and for safe routine – to allow your daughter to test herself and develop resilience in a wide range of life's arenas.

Your daughter will learn not only from what she does, but also from your reactions to what she does. She will learn when she talks to you about what you think and feel, and this will help her to consider what she herself thinks and feels in relation to these thoughts, ideas and emotions.

She will learn from her peers and from other female role models, all the time comparing what they think and feel with her own thoughts and feelings, while reaching a deeper understanding of herself. You can help her on this journey by talking with her and listening to her. In today's world, possibly the most important qualities that your daughter can learn to develop are:

* flexibility
* creative thinking
* the ability to seek out, find and make the most of opportunities

All of these qualities require a certain degree of resilience. She will develop this from experience and from the support she receives from you and from others.

One of the most important lessons you can teach her is the ability to pick herself up after a fall – either literal or metaphorical. A word of wisdom, however: the most significant thing about your daughter's self-discovery is that it is precisely that – discovery by your daughter on her own to work out who she is.

You naturally want the best for your daughter, and don't want to see her 'waste' her life. You want your daughter – for any number of reasons – either to take a different path from your own, or to follow in your footsteps, and almost certainly to do better than you did.

If you are not careful, you may judge your daughter according to what you yourself want, and not according to what she might want and need. This is the real leap that parents need to take. Your daughter is a unique creation, combining qualities, ideas and behaviours that you may well recognise from yourself or other members of your family, but in a way that is entirely individual to her. If you are not careful, there is the possibility that you may make her journey more difficult, trying to fit her into a mould that doesn't work for her, hampering her self-development and the growth of understanding about herself.

This doesn't mean that you can't do anything to support your daughter on her way – it just means that you have to remain honest and self-aware. It also means that you can't always make her do what you want her to do – a lesson no doubt learnt during the days of those toddler tantrums!

Girls and risk-taking

Girls are not natural risk-takers. Often they worry far too much about 'getting it wrong' and, as a result, play things safe. Responsible parents and good schools encourage girls to take risks within a safe and structured environment, learning that no one will think any the less of them if they make a mistake. The underlying message needs to be: 'Come on in; the water's warm.'

We all recognise that healthy self-esteem is the key to confidence and success if we want our children to feel good about themselves. The crux of healthy self-esteem is that you should feel both capable and lovable. Girls tend to undersell themselves and be overly self-critical. Boys, conversely, can have a tendency to overestimate their abilities. Girls who are bright, talented and attractive can still have a negative self-image. A perfectionist tendency can cause girls to judge themselves harshly and to see anything less than perfection in themselves as unacceptable.

You can encourage your daughter to recognise this tendency and to resist the urge to aim constantly for perfection and to beat herself up if she doesn't attain it. Encourage her to be brave, resilient and realistic.

You can foster healthy self-esteem in your daughter, but praise and reassurance alone won't achieve this. In particular, empty praise will achieve only cynicism and distrust. In order to boost her self-esteem realistically, you need to help her to see her strengths and positive qualities, which may be social and emotional rather than narrowly academic.

Having identified her strengths (and she needs to be the one to make this identification, rather than you doing it for her), you can encourage her to develop her talents, set challenges for herself and take risks. When she meets a challenge that is realistic but demanding, attempting it will cause her to feel better about herself, and her self-esteem will increase. Show faith in her, stand by her and listen to her.

Help her to face and deal with disappointment and share in her joy when she achieves something she didn't think possible.

Consider the following platitudes:

- If we don't risk failure, we never achieve success.
- Failure lies not in falling down but in not getting up.

Encourage your daughter to take a risk – and watch her blossom.

Are girls growing up too fast?

What can parents do about it?

We live in a relatively uncensored society, where it can be easy to find and gain access to highly sexualised films, books, magazines and other media. Much of what passes for 'normal' comment about women and girls in our daily newspapers often focuses, at least to some extent, on appearance and perceived attractiveness. Is it therefore any surprise that girls are often encouraged to grow up too quickly, aspiring to look and act and feel like adults before they have perhaps developed the judgement to balance out their feelings and behaviour?

Rather than simply accepting this, however, parents should understand that it is their role to establish limits and boundaries, and to ensure that, as much as possible, their daughters are exposed only to age-appropriate material. Parents need to be honest in this – we cannot pretend that our daughters will never grow up, never reach puberty or never experience emerging feelings of sexuality. We cannot keep them children for ever, and nor can we entirely protect them from images and ideas that they will encounter in society. We can, however, help them along the path if we are sensible in our approach.

Practical tips and strategies

Be aware of what particular images, toys and games represent, and don't bow to pressure if you feel that what your daughter wants is inappropriately sexualised. Lap-dancing kits and 'sexy' underwear for 7-year-olds are never going to be entirely harmless in the messages they communicate.

Read what your daughter is reading, and watch what she is watching. If you are shocked by what you see (and you might be, if you read some of the magazines aimed at pre- and young teens), then talk to your daughter and tell her how you feel. Explore why she is reading this – is it because her friends read this? If so, sharing your moral position with her, and the fact that you are unafraid to hold it, may give her courage to do something different.

Listen to your daughter and deal sensitively with her. If it is embarrassing for you to talk about sex, then it is ten times worse for her. If you want to draw her to you, then don't be put off if she tries to avoid talking about it.

Growing up — practical support strategies

You can't tell your daughter who and what she will be in life, or do her self-discovering for her, but as a parent, you have a vital role to play in helping your daughter along the way. In your role as parent, you can give her plenty of help and guidance.

The jury on the nature/nurture debate may be out still, but you have helped to form your daughter's character and can make a pretty good guess at understanding what she is feeling as she moves through some of the difficulties of growing up.

Work out what you felt like when you were younger. How do you react now? This should help to give you a greater understanding of your daughter. If you understand, it will show and she will feel more secure.

A supportive, loving environment is essential to self-esteem and gives a stable rock from which she can explore her inner and outer worlds. Your daughter needs to know that she can take risks, make mistakes, and even fail, and that she will always be able to come back to you. She needs to know that you love her even when she believes that she has 'failed'.

The one thing your daughter needs from you is time. You can't always give this but try to give as much as you can. Time allows space for discussion, for questions to emerge and to be answered and for a reaffirmation to your daughter that you are always there for her. Car journeys, meal times, chores – all these give opportunities for 'casual' chats.

And if all of this seems rather passive, the final thing you can do for your daughter is to provide opportunities. The more opportunities your daughter has and the more exposure she has to different activities and events, the better able she will be to know what is 'out there'.

Opportunities that you can provide include:

- **Female role models and networks:** Girls learn from their mothers, other female family members and from other female role models. The lifelong friendships and networks that girls and young women develop are invaluable in supporting them as they move through their lives.
- **Education:** A good school is much more than just lessons and preparation for qualifications – a good school will form the basis of friendship groups and will have tremendous opportunities for clubs, activities, trips and events.
- **Facilitating your daughter's passion:** You can go a long way to help develop your daughter's interests, within the bounds of what is practical, affordable and possible, of course!
- **Outings and visits:** Seeing different things and meeting different people will allow your daughter to expand her world view and understanding of her place within it.
- **Voluntary work and community service:** From helping out with siblings at an early age to volunteering in the community in her late teens, your daughter will benefit from taking responsibility and learning how to deal with other people.
- **Aiming high:** Helping your daughter to understand her ambitions and motivations and to set goals and values is important in life. Your daughter will have absorbed many of her values from those around her, but she will develop her own value system based on the influences she encounters in the course of her life journey. Discuss with her what matters to you and to her, as this will help her to understand her own values more clearly.

Values underpin our motivations, and it is your daughter's own motivations that will help to propel her into choosing life goals – both short and long-term. Identifying goals and working out how to reach them is a sure-fire step towards success in any area of life.

Girls benefit from setting clear goals. If you have ongoing discussions with your daughter about what she feels, what she believes in and what she might like to achieve in life, then you can help to encourage her to set these goals. A word of warning, however: you cannot give her the motivation, nor can you set the goals for her. By encouraging your daughter to think about her values and motivations, and by taking the opportunity to talk to her about them, you can help her to clarify her thoughts about what she herself wants to achieve.

GROWING UP

Thoughts from a Head – having it all

You may have read a story about Cambridge female under-graduates posing scantily clad, which led to media stories about 'bluestockings and bimbos'. Girls can be highly intel-ligent and interested in being seen to be attractive – the two aren't mutually exclusive. Caring about physical appear-ance and fashion and wanting to feel good about how you look doesn't have to be a betrayal of some feminist ideal. I love new shoes, but it doesn't make me shallow. Girls can have fun and also be taken seriously.

We hope our girls' education, within the classroom and beyond it, will give them a range of options and a positive self-image so that they stretch and challenge themselves and then feel proud of all they achieve, without expecting to be perfect at everything and feeling guilty if they don't manage to be Wonderwoman.

A member of my staff gave me a copy of an article from the *Independent* that listed girls' and boys' career aspirations at age 11 and 16 sixty years ago, compared with their aspirations in the early twenty-first century. Sixty years ago, boys chose as their dream professions jobs such as train driver, racing driver, mechanic, fireman. Girls chose professions such as nurse, air stewardess, hairdresser, ballerina. In the twenty-first century poll, boys' top choice was footballer (at age 11) and a job in IT (at 16). Girls' top choices included fashion designer, lawyer, doctor, optician, physiotherapist, and the top choice, at both ages 11 and 16, was vet.

This was echoed in an article by Alice Thomson in *The Times*. She returned to her former school to present prizes and was taken aback at how girls' aspirations had developed since she attended the school only as far back as the 1980s. She said: 'When I went back, prepared to give a stirring speech to the pupils about reaching their potential, I realised they had already exceeded anything I'd ever done. I discovered that many of them already had ten starred As at GCSE, their gold Duke of Edinburgh's Awards, had set up their own internet businesses, won medals for debating, were competing for Britain in sailing and had grade 8 distinction on the oboe. As they staggered away with their booty, it was clear they were already thinking of becoming editors or economists, brain surgeons or barristers.' But she then goes on to say, 'What they hadn't realised is that while they are probably even more talented than their male contemporaries, their lives will be different, more complicated and maybe also more complete. What I wish I'd known at 18 was that while I could possibly become a chief executive, I might also want to be a mother, that I might not want to work flat-out, full-time for 40 years to reach the top, that woman + work is an easy equation to balance, but adding a baby into the sum turns it into a conundrum.'

In addition to their professional aspirations, currently four-fifths of women have children. Sixty per cent of UK mothers return to work within six months of having a child – a very small proportion now stay at home until the child reaches school age. That may be financially driven to some degree, but it's one of the facts of life for which we have to prepare our girls. We know that generally the girls in our schools want demanding careers rather than just jobs, and given that the vast majority of them will choose to have families, too, they have a challenging future ahead. If they leave us expecting to be the perfect wife, perfect mother and perfect Chief Executive, we haven't prepared them for the reality of this challenging future. But if we give them the confidence to achieve their best and feel proud of that, whatever it might be; not to feel unduly guilty if they cannot be all things to all people; to be able to work in partnership with others and to make full use of the support they have available to them; to have the self-assurance to exercise choice – at certain stages of their lives they will have different priorities and what they choose at one time will not be the same as what they choose at another time – but it should be a choice, and a choice they feel comfortable with.

There was a superb article in the *Observer* written by Gaby Hinsliff, the paper's political editor, entitled, 'I had it all, but I didn't have a life' about her decision to resign in order to spend more time with her 2-year-old son. It describes the dilemma many of our girls will face – in fact, which many of our high-achieving staff, and the Heads in our schools face, when they combine a demanding professional life with parenthood. If we manage to educate our girls so that they are capable of dealing with this dilemma when the time comes, then we will have done well by them. It is all about balance. Many of our girls want it all. I think our job is to prepare them as well as we can to cope with the complexities and the challenge of the balancing act they will inevitably face in the future. To an extent we do this in our schools when we offer them a huge range of opportunities and they find even at junior school age that they can't do the recorder and netball and choir all during the same lunchtime. They have to learn, with our support, about pacing themselves, about commitment, about being realistic in their expectations of themselves — aim high, but don't make yourself miserable by trying to do everything and aiming for perfection in everything. We also need to prepare girls who will ultimately become mothers themselves for the responsibility of being positive role models for their own children.

My sixth form girls this year had the opportunity to enter an essay competition in which they wrote about who they thought were important female role models in the twenty-first century. They wrote about politicians, sports stars, pioneers in different fields — but by far the most commonly quoted role model was the individual writer's mother. Because these were 17–18-year-old girls, these were usually working mothers, and the comments the girls made about their admiration for their working mothers reminded me of a comment I read by the daughter of a journalist who's also a single parent, in the *Daily Mail* in September. The daughter, Alice Chunn, said, 'From a young age I have carried with me a fierce sense of pride about my mother's impressive career. I would be proud to follow in her footsteps. She has had a demanding professional life while raising three children. Not only do I love my mother but I respect her, and not just because she is my mother but because of all she has achieved.' We need to educate our girls so if they choose to be working mothers, they need to get a grip on their guilt. If they choose not to work and to stay at home with their children, at least for a period of time, they shouldn't feel guilty. If they choose not to have children at all, they shouldn't feel guilty. If they find they are unable to have children, that's also something we need to educate them to be able to handle. That's what I wish for the girls we are responsible for educating.

Teaching girls patience in a world of instant gratification

It's enough to drive a parent to distraction: you're trudging round the supermarket doing the weekly shop, when suddenly your toddler spots her favourite sweets and moves swiftly from asking to begging to roaring and screaming! And it doesn't get any easier as she gets older – the right clothes, the 'in' toys and gadgets, to go anywhere anytime with anyone . . . It's what she wants and she wants it now.

The messages she absorbs from the media and from her friends are that she 'deserves' what she wants, that she should have it when she wants it – so how, or indeed who, are you to persuade her otherwise? The satisfaction of knowing something has been achieved to the best of one's ability enhances personal esteem, but in today's world of instant communication, fast food, instant gratification and the global village, this 'pleasure' is hard to describe and can be lost in the reality of daily life. Equally hard to describe is the notion that 'actions have consequences' and that hard work does eventually bring its own rewards.

The following are some examples of pop psychology exercises assessing emotional intelligence. In describing several typical scenarios, each with its own multiple choice answers, it is relatively easy to make a teenager think about her response to a situation:

Q: You want to go out with your friends on Saturday night. You have already arranged to go out with a different group on Friday. Your exams are in four weeks' time. You ask your mum, and she says no. Do you?

a. Slam the door and sulk in your bedroom.

b. Make the arrangements anyway – as if you didn't hear her.

c. Try to make her feel unreasonable: 'I'm never allowed to do anything.'

d. Ask your dad.

e. Convince both parents you will not go out the following weekend.

Clearly, the emotionally mature answer is 'e', to negotiate your way out of a difficulty. But the thought-provoking alternatives allow a teenager to both laugh at herself and realise the value of the exercise. Try altering the question to apply to an adult work situation, and the teenager can see that the practice of emotionally mature behaviour will help her in later life:

Q: You want to leave work early next Friday. You have already arranged to leave early this Friday. Your end of year financial report is due in four weeks' time. You ask your boss, and she says no. Do you?

a. Slam the door and sulk in your office.

b. Make the arrangements anyway – as if you didn't hear her.

c. Try to make her feel unreasonable: 'I'm never allowed to do anything.'

d. Ask her boss.

e. Convince your boss that you will not ask to leave early again until your report is complete.

Children are, of course, great imitators – your daughter will copy you in most things, including whether you work hard and wait patiently to attain your goals. If you model the behaviour you want her to emulate, you have every chance of raising your daughter to value most those things she works and waits for. The premise that life will bring increased rewards with delayed gratification is the basis of our whole national educational system, and the clearer we make the message, the better understood it will be!

Dealing with disappointment

It is the business of schools to celebrate success: it's in our newsletters, school magazines and prize-giving reports. Our mission statements imply that everyone can have success, that this is what they should aspire to and when they do achieve it, we give them the tokens of success: badges and certificates; cups and medals and prizes; and we heap congratulations on them, often very publicly.

There are so many things to which we encourage our students to aspire: A* grades and scholarships; a leading part in the school play; to sing a solo in the concert; to captain the netball team; to be selected for the county; to be chosen for a school exchange; to be appointed as head girl; to be the best public speaker; to win an essay competition. And when our daughters and students achieve one of these successes, we are thrilled for them because to be the best feels great and is a vindication of all their efforts.

But what of the occasions – and there will be many – when the girls we are responsible for do not succeed, when their effort and ambition are met by disappointment and even despair at a dream dashed? Supporting our young people through disappointment is every bit as important as supporting them to achieve success. In fact, if we don't manage to do the former, they may never go on to enjoy the latter.

Readers may feel that the problem is being exaggerated. After all, we learn to deal early on with the toddler who wants something they can't have and, in some ways, disappointment is not dissimilar: we can't always be first or best. But there are two ways in which disappointment (or fear of it) in our girls can present a genuine challenge to parents and teachers.

Firstly, there is the girl who puts her 'all' into preparation for selection of, say, a school or county team, a leading part or a position of responsibility. In spite of her very best efforts, she doesn't make the cut. Many others in her position may be philosophical, saying, 'Next time, maybe.' But your daughter is stunned by the outcome; she can't understand what more she could have done, she doesn't believe the girl who has been selected ahead of her is really any better than she is (and frankly, neither do you); she cannot understand why she wasn't the one. She cries and cries; she is distraught, bewildered, furious and then she cries again. She vows she will never try anything like this in future; it's not fair, she never gets anything!

As parents and teachers, we need to remember that disappointment can be like grief: an almost physical pain that threatens to be all-consuming. It is therefore important not to underestimate it, nor should we allow our daughters to wallow in it. The following ideas are drawn from some excellent advice from an educational psychologist to a group of parents and teachers.

The first tip is to allow space for a young person's feelings. Yes, they feel acutely upset and disappointed. Yes, they can't understand why they didn't succeed. Yes, they feel awful, tearful, dejected. If your daughter is telling you how she feels, just nod and agree with her. Don't (as is very natural) try to dismiss or disagree with her feelings, however much you want to convince her that she is talented and capable. It is really important not to contradict her (for example, 'Darling, it doesn't matter. I still think you are wonderful'). Of course it matters – she may have been looking forward to this for weeks and weeks. And the selection panel obviously doesn't think she's wonderful, or they would have chosen her and that's what matters! So resist the desire to contradict and reassure her. Instead, just listen. So, listen hard and acknowledge what she is feeling by nodding and making noises of agreement and understanding. And then, however counter-intuitive this may seem, confirm her feelings with 'You must be feeling really disappointed', 'You must feel like your effort has not been recognised' and then try something that articulates what she was hoping for, 'I expect you wish they would still select you', 'I expect you wish you had the part instead of Jenny.'

Such a conversation simply acknowledges how your daughter is feeling and shows her that you realise how upset she is, rather than trying to cheer her up or make her see it differently or change her feelings. The final stage is really empowering. Don't tell her what to do next. Instead, ask her what she is going to do: 'What do you think you will do now?' 'Is there anything you can do about this?' 'Will you speak to anyone about this?' 'Is there anything I can do to help you?'

After the initial experience of disappointment, our job as parents and teachers is to help our girls to move on. They will get over disappointment, especially if we let them by diverting them with new topics of conversation and keeping away from the sensitive issues unless they themselves raise them.

Because we know through experience how painful disappointment can be, it would be easy to conspire unconsciously with some girls' natural aversion to risk-taking. This is the other great challenge presented by instances of our girls' disappointment. Why encourage her to try for the school play or to take the scholarship exam, knowing how many other talented girls are trying and how unlikely she is to succeed. Why put her through it? The answer is, of course, obvious, though it is by no means easy. It is essential that we each learn to take risks and that we are willing to face the possibility of disappointment, otherwise we will never make progress and learn new things. In fact, it is our job as parents and teachers to encourage our girls and young women into new and challenging experiences in the full knowledge that failure will sometimes happen and bring pain, but that it is also an inevitable and necessary building block for future success.

Thoughts from a Head — the parenting challenge

Parenting is a challenge — but don't take the joy out of it. We also want to be able to turn our children into superstars while raising them to be rounded and grounded . . .

All children have specific traits and characteristics that will predispose them towards certain forms of achievement or growth. As parents, one of our major roles is to spend time observing and understanding our children as they grow and develop, to try to assess who they are deep down. Our understanding will grow as they grow, as long as we are acutely aware of them for who they are.

As parents, we often bring our own agenda to our children's lives, and this is difficult to avoid. We want them to be different from who we were and are, or to follow in our footsteps. Almost certainly, we want them to have better opportunities than we had, and to become more successful than we did. There is nothing wrong with this, but there is a lot wrong with the rest. If we seek to impose our own expectations on our children, we risk undermining their growth. They are who they are, not necessarily who we want them to be, and our role as parents is to recognise this and to encourage their growth.

In fact, we are aiming for something quite general but equally quite spectacular. Your child may be particularly gifted in music, languages, sport, drama, maths or art, but unless they grow an inner confidence and self-esteem and we find a way to help them achieve this, they are not going to attain the inner contentment we know they need to see them through. If we can help them to be free from self-imposed limitations and to believe in themselves, they will have a bright future ahead of them, with the world at their feet. If you recognise your child's interests and passions and provide the right opportunities, you can go a long way to help facilitate them, allowing your child to deepen their experiences, thereby enriching their lives.

Outings and visits are important, too. Seeing different things and meeting different people will allow your child to expand their world view and understanding of their place within it. Voluntary work and community service are also a tremendous opportunity In teaching your child responsibility and understanding of others.

You can, of course, take the notion of opportunities too far — and this will be counter-productive if you do so. Occasionally, parents can bow to competitive pressure to schedule in as much as possible into their children's lives, rushing them from ballet, to French, to extra maths, in an attempt to cram in as many experiences and as much learning as possible. 'Why play when you can learn?' seems to be the mantra on many parents' lips today, squeezing as many extra classes into the day as possible. The truth is, of course,

GROWING UP

that our children learn through play and need time just to learn to be themselves. Does your 3-year-old have a diary? If so, bin it! Overorganisation and relentless scheduling leave no time for a child to breathe, and having the space and time to do nothing — just to think and grow — are essential to a child's development.

Education — the choice of school — is one of the biggest opportunities we can give to our children. You are looking for a school that will match your child's needs, where your child will feel comfortable, happy, ready to be inspired and somewhere people genuinely care about the individual for who she is.

In this, time is important. The single most important piece of advice in the raising of superstars is this: spend time with your children. It is one of the greatest gifts we can give to them — time to be together, time to listen, time to laugh, time to share, time to relax, time just to be and to do nothing. Time is precious for all of us, but setting time aside for our children is absolutely invaluable for their growth.

Life is full of uncertainty and unexpected occurrences. Rather than viewing these as a problem, we should understand how important it is that we build up resilience in our children by allowing them to experience many unexpected and challenging new environments. As parents, we cannot choose the people our children will encounter at school and in the wider world, but we can observe, be aware, help explain how others think and behave and encourage our children to grow as a result.

One of the essential truths is that a child's development is rarely a linear, bump-free process. It will go up and down; just when you think they should need you less, they need you more; just when they think they need more independence, you might realise that they need more boundaries. Don't be surprised by this; embrace it! Raising a child is a lengthy and time-consuming process. Hard though it is to let go, it is what we are destined to do as parents, and the absolute fulfilment of our role comes when our child grows up. There is a glorious moment of achievement when you recognise that your child has a rich grounding and can happily be her own individual.

Fortunately, or unfortunately, there is no such thing as the perfect parent. In truth, it is usually in the recognition of our own inadequacies and faith in our children for who they are that the best parenting actually occurs.

Growing up Q&A

A question of trust — an issue with teenagers
Q: My 15-year-old daughter now has an extensive network of friends extending across various schools (thanks to Facebook). This has resulted in increased pressure from her to 'do' the things that they (apparently) are allowed to do, and we have trusted her with some of these activities but not allowed her to do others (e.g. staying out at 11 pm in the local woods). A recent event (which could involve the police) revealed that our daughter has systematically lied to us about everything she has been doing and where she has been. She continues not to tell us the truth. How can I persuade her that honesty is always the best policy?

A: This is one of those situations in which you need to be firm, strong and very, very clear with your daughter. At best, she has twisted the truth and been misguided in her friendships; at worst, she has put herself into very real danger, and you need to show her this. One of the most important things we teach our children is that actions have consequences. She has lied to you, and the consequence of this is that now you cannot trust her to do what she says she is doing, until she has proven that she can be trusted again.

You should consider restricting her outings, activities, allowance and access to the internet, phone, etc., with immediate effect — she needs to realise again that you are the parent in your relationship and that you have the capacity to require her to act and behave in certain ways for her own good. If this sounds rather draconian, remember that you are not doing this in perpetuity, and, of course, explain to her why you are doing this. However, you do need to re-establish the boundaries within which she can live and play safely, and she may need this shock to let her see how close she has come to damaging herself, her future and her life.

You have most likely already had many of these conversations, and you may not feel as though they have any effect, but do persist. It is very possible to say to our children that we love them deeply, but that we do not like what they are doing, nor will we accept it, and these messages do hit home, although don't expect your daughter suddenly to see the errors of her ways, or, in fact, to want to do things exactly the way you want her to. There will still be negotiation and discussion, and, certainly, you need to allow her to be able to redeem herself and start out afresh, but you need to make the boundaries very, very clear. Truth, honesty and safety — these are essentials on which you cannot compromise.

If it is any consolation at all, you are not alone in this. Teenagers have to test rules and boundaries to help them to establish who they are, and every parent will have a similar or related experience at some point. This said, it is our role as parents and schools to make sure that we bring our experience to bear in showing our children the right direction. It is a hard and often thankless task in the short – and even medium – term, but it will be worth it eventually.

Teenagers and staying up late

Q: I know that when the school year starts again in a couple of weeks, I will have the normal battle with my 14-year-old daughter about her bedtime. Last term on a school night her bedtime was 9 pm, being allowed a further 15 minutes to read (and nothing else) before lights out. She says this is too early and her friends stay up later – but believe me, she needs her sleep. At weekends and holidays her bedtime is extended by about an hour but never any later than 10.30; again she says it is too early. I am wondering if you could offer any advice or if there are any guidelines laid down for such issues and if you think I am being unreasonable? Just a thought, do boarding schools have a set bedtime for each year group or do they all differ?

A: The Head of Boarding at one of the leading girls' independent schools says their Year 9s go to bed at 9.30pm, with lights out at 9.45pm. Year 10s go 15 minutes later, and Year 11s are 15 minutes after that. Their sixth form have to be quiet and in their rooms by 11 pm. Boarders are reminded that because they're busy all day working, singing, playing, talking, etc., they need to have sufficient sleep to do the same again the next day. Perhaps you could share this information with your daughter. The Head added, 'Enforcing a bedtime strictly is not sensible, any more than "forcing" a girl to study or to eat. Overall, I'm sure the girls are not asleep at lights out but I estimate that most nights most girls are sleeping within half an hour of that.'

It is so important to encourage girls to take care of themselves and to develop good habits of eating, sleeping and exercising. All parents are told that 'all my friends' go to bed later, get more pocket money, are allowed out more, etc., and that's probably what we told our own parents! But parents' responsibility is to guide their children until they are sufficiently mature to act responsibly themselves.

Pushing the boundaries

Q: My 12-year-old daughter is leading me to the end of my tether. She has always been fiery, but the last few months it has been getting worse. My partner and I have tried all ways with her — from grounding her and taking away all privileges, to allowing her to do 'what she wants' within reason. She slams doors, throws things around and talks to us like we are beneath her and owe her something! I don't know what to do anymore and most nights sit in tears, although I will not show her how she makes me feel. I tell her I love her, hug her and if she does well at school, praise her. Please help me.

A: It is always a bit of a shock when children start to behave in ways that seem alien and entirely at odds with the person we thought they were becoming — that nice linear progression from baby to toddler to well-adjusted young person. Such are the realities of the early teenage years, and it is important to take comfort from the fact that this is entirely normal. With the onset of puberty, so many changes are taking place in a young person's body, from hormones to brain growth, that it is unsurprising they can feel out of control, and often subconsciously fearful and anxious, and that this can translate into extremely challenging behaviour.

The first step for parents is to recognise this, and to prepare as well as possible to have to hand the necessary resources, the most important of which is patience. This phase will last some time, and you will need the strength to recognise that it is not your fault, but rather a natural process. Make sure that you have enough time for yourself so that you can be measured in your approach to your daughter. This does not mean, however, that you should be relaxed in allowing her to behave however she wants; on the contrary, she needs boundaries now more than ever before. Think of her as a toddler again — a very apt analogy, because she is now exploring the capacities of her new, growing and changing mind and body, which are all strange to her. Do think carefully about these boundaries, though — she needs boundaries to keep her safe and well, but will need the space to explore in other ways, too, so rules that you used to have may no longer be appropriate. Decide which are the important rules and be very consistent — if she breaks them, then she has to know what the consequences will be, and you must follow through.

Above all, take every opportunity to praise your daughter and to show her that you love her. Don't expect this to necessarily be reciprocated at this stage — but it will strike home. And do enlist the help of many other people, as teenagers need a range of adult mentors to help give them guidance, understand the world around them and to find their place within it. Talk to your daughter's school — you may find that she is a model pupil — but sharing the experiences that you are having at home will help the school to look for ways to support your daughter emotionally. This is not failure as a parent — on the contrary, it takes a village to raise a child, and if you are facilitating this, then you are doing something very positive for your daughter.

One suggestion is to read Ken and Elizabeth Mellor's excellent book, *Teen Stages*, in which the authors describe a range of positive strategies to help guide your early teenager through the next few years. Don't be put off by the fact that they attribute the stages to slightly older ages (e.g. 13–14); girls grow up quickly now, and you are wise to be a step ahead. Parenting a teenager — from early to late stages — is probably one of the most challenging tasks we ever face.

My 7-year-old won't stop whining

Q: My 7-year-old whines as soon as something doesn't go her way. We have tried the teacher's ideas of playing games so she understands that sometimes she loses, ignoring it and punishing it, and even suggesting other things to take her mind off it. All to no avail, and once the whining starts, it is non-stop for the rest of the day. My 3-year-old daughter is now starting to copy her sister's behaviour. Please help before I have two like this.

A: This may be one of those situations where you are going to have to grit your teeth and bear it for a little while longer. You will probably find it intensely irritating, and hard to deal with — in a war of attrition, however, you can win if you put your efforts into remaining calm, not reacting and staying utterly consistent. Plan your strategy and stick with it — the teacher's ideas are absolutely right, but will need a lot of implementation if they are to become embedded with your daughter, particularly as she will have seen by now how much she is capable of irritating you. Start from the principle that not everything will go her way, and she needs to realise this (hence, the game-playing); moreover, whining is inappropriate behaviour and you will not tolerate it. This means that when she whines, she can expect you to react in certain disapproving ways that she will not enjoy — all of the strategies of ignoring and sanctions, for instance. The real trick, however, is for you to not react with anger or irritation — control your feelings, and you will deprive her of the reaction she has been seeking. The behaviour will soon change when she realises this.

Should my 11-year-old read teenage magazines?
Q: I have forbidden my daughter to buy teenage magazines, as I worry about her growing up too soon. Have I done the right thing? She is only 11 years old.

A: It is very normal for you to be concerned about whether your daughter is growing up too fast, but it is also normal for her to be curious about her next stage of development and eager to be 'grown-up'. Girls are growing up quicker, and your daughter is beginning to experience many changes to her brain and her body, and the range of emotions that these changes bring. As she experiences the onset of puberty, you will need to establish boundaries that will help to keep her healthy and safe. It is crucial that you decide which rules you can enforce and which are most important — then stick to them.

With this in mind, reflect on your decision to forbid her

GROWING UP

165

buying magazines designed for teenage girls. Most likely, she will be able to read her friends' copies but may not tell you the truth about whether she is reading them outside the home. You may decide that you would rather she brought these magazines home so you can read them and discuss the content with her. Perhaps you could read one or two examples first so you can guide her. You may find yourself surprisingly reassured by how responsible many of the articles are and you can explain to her what your reservations are about others. Guiding children through their teenage years isn't easy but it can be very rewarding, and open communication is the key to success

I suspect my 13-year-old is shoplifting

Q: What should I do if I suspect that my 13-year-old is shoplifting?

A: Firstly, try to work out whether your suspicions are justified — can you find evidence? Do try to do so if you have strong suspicions, as it is always far better (although not impossible) to begin a discussion when you have clear proof that your daughter has taken something that she shouldn't have. With a stolen object on the table, your daughter will not be able to escape the consequences of her actions, and it is really important that she is made to face them, if she is to be dissuaded from this path in the future. She may have shoplifted because of peer pressure, or because she was testing rules, or for the thrill. Regardless of the reason, you need to show her that her actions have consequences, and potentially very serious ones, especially if she does it again. You should impose sanctions — perhaps removing her allowance for a while, or preventing her from going out for a certain amount of time; you should also seriously consider arranging for her to take back the item or items she has stolen. Having to face up to the realities of what she has done will be extremely sobering for her, and may be the wake-up call she needs. It will be hard for you, too, but as parents if we don't insist upon enforcing these sorts of boundaries, then we send a message to our children that they are not important. Moreover, as teenagers need to test boundaries in order to help to define who they are, we risk encouraging them to test ever-more dangerous options. You need to be firm and absolutely unequivocal — shoplifting is wrong, and she must never, ever do it again.

Q: My teenage daughter doesn't seem to be very interested in anything. How can I help her to develop an interest?

A: Be honest with yourself first of all — to what extent are you trying to turn her into someone she isn't? If you can satisfy yourself that this is not the case, then try to establish why she isn't displaying a great deal of interest in life. Is she lacking in self-esteem, for instance? Perhaps she needs you to provide a wider range of opportunities for her? Don't be frustrated if she doesn't seem to take up anything you suggest — just keep going and keep being encouraging. She needs to understand that you feel that it is safe for her to fail before she will take risks. Don't rule out a physical cause for her lack of interest: as a growing child, her minerals, vitamins and hormones may be out of kilter, and if you are worried, you should take her to see the family GP. Above all, though, listen to her and seek to understand her; and then be as supportive as you can.

Q: *My daughter is coming to the end of her time at school and still doesn't know what she wants to do in life. How can I help to give her a direction?*

A: The truth is that you can't — but you can help her to see that she has all sorts of exciting opportunities ahead of her. Try to see it positively: as she grows, the more self-aware she becomes, and the more likely it is that she will choose a job and way of life that is best suited to her. Careers are rarely for life these days, and there is an enormous amount of flexibility within the job market. Continue encouraging her to think, and keep giving her opportunities to meet with people and talk to them about their jobs, careers and lives, and she will find her own direction in good time.

Q: *My daughter is finding it difficult to settle at her new school. I don't know what to do to help her. Do you have any tips?*

A: The first thing you need to try to establish is exactly why is she unsettled and unhappy. If this is a house move and she is coping with a lot of change, the issue may be just general adjustment and not specifically to do with school (although she may feel it is). If she has moved from one type of school to another (for example, from primary to secondary school), it may be the size of the school and the difference in routines, such as having so many different teachers and needing to take increased responsibility for personal organisation, which she is finding challenging. Does she feel out of her depth academically, and thus may need more support with schoolwork? Or is this all about friendships, which girls tend to feel considerably more anxious about than boys at this stage? It is important that you encourage your daughter to talk about exactly when she feels at her most anxious – is it the journey to school? Deciding who to sit with and talk to when she arrives each day? How she spends her break and lunchtime? Homework? Once you have ascertained this, talk to the school staff and enlist their support. If they are aware of exactly how she is feeling, they will be better able to help her – perhaps by allocating her a 'buddy', an individual pupil who can take particular responsibility for looking after her until she has found her feet. Don't give up – and don't be tempted to let her stay home to avoid the problem. With both your support and that of the school, she can get through this.

Q: My daughter has fallen in with the wrong crowd and we constantly argue about this. How can I get through to her?

A: You need to be able to identify why you feel this is the 'wrong crowd' and to try to see how your daughter's perception, and yours, might differ. How well do you know her friends and is there any way you can get to know them better? If you do so and you still feel they have a negative influence on her, all you can do is to explain to your daughter, as unemotionally as you can, the nature of your concerns. If her friendship with the group is making her unhappy or putting her at risk in some way, then she may be receptive to what you have to say. If neither of these is true, then ask yourself why you are so worried. Difficult though it may be to accept, parents can't dictate their children's friendship choices, much as they might like to. This is her life and she has to make her own decisions – and sometimes her own mistakes. All a loving and responsible parent can do, like a good school, is to give children a framework within which to make these choices, decisions and mistakes, and to support them when they get things wrong. You will love her regardless; just make sure she knows this.

Q: My daughter has told me that one of her friends is self-harming. What should I say to her?

A: Praise her for coming to you. Ask her if she has talked to this friend about why she is doing this to herself. Suggest that she tells a teacher, in confidence, because a teacher will have experience of how to help. Even if it seems like the most direct approach, don't contact the girl's parents directly. If your daughter is unwilling to tell a teacher herself, then you should talk to the Head.

Educating

In today's competitive world a good education is essential. You start teaching your daughter from the first few weeks onward but then you face decisions: stay at home to raise her? Child minder or au pair or granny? Nursery or playgroup? Local state school or an independent school? Single sex or co-ed, day or boarding?

There is a Chinese saying that it takes a whole village to raise a child but here it will be you and her school that will educate her, so choosing the right one for your daughter is important. Children learn best when they are happy and girls in particular need to be emotionally engaged to assimilate knowledge and acquire new skills. Your daughter may benefit from different solutions at different stages of her life so the school you choose for her when she's 5 may not provide what she needs at 11. You should consider her personality and temperament, her developing interest and talents. And then you will want to support her: to help her to learn; to work with her school; to encourage, reassure, support and direct her.

Under 5s

As your daughter grows from a newborn to a pre-school toddler, she will develop at a faster rate than at any other stage in her life. You will want to cuddle and feed her, to show her the exciting world she is learning about and, in the early days, to sleep! You will face many choices and take many decisions, from when to wean her to whether she should go to nursery, perhaps whether you should or could return to work and how to prepare her for when she starts school. There are many sources of support for you: family and friends; health professionals; books; magazines and, of course, the internet. Try not to get overwhelmed. Remember that generations of children have grown up despite,

171

as well as because of, their parents! Trust your instincts; as her parent you have a head start on everyone else and, above all, enjoy these early years, as they fly by.

Under 5s — education choices

The early years education continues to receive considerable media attention. Talk of a 'toddler curriculum' with goals and targets contributes to parents' anxiety about how and where their young children should begin their educational journey.

Some parents will begin to consider these issues before their child is even born, particularly if there is a high demand for nursery places in the area and they expect to return to work. Whether or not you return to work, and where and how your daughter will be cared for if you do, will be very significant decisions for the family. Advice abounds and you may be surprised by the passion with which otherwise mild-mannered and well-meaning friends and relations will put across their view of what's best for your child. Always remember that it is your child you are dealing with and that you are the one who has to live and work with the decisions you make on a daily basis – trust your instincts.

For some families needing childcare, a nanny will be the answer; for others, a childminder; and for others, a nursery. In many cases, a combination of care will be best – one day a week with grandma, two days at nursery and two days with mum or dad, who is now working part-time or flexibly.

It will always be a question of juggling priorities, so ask yourself a few questions:

- Is it important to you that your daughter is cared for in her own home or by a family member?
- Do you want your daughter to learn to socialise with other children as early as possible?

- Is your daughter a confident, outgoing child who loves new experiences, or is she more home-loving and reserved with strangers?

The government's public service website has helpful information for parents on all aspects of childcare and the National Day Nurseries Association, the National Childminding Association, and the parenting section of the BBC website, all offer insights and assistance with finding appropriate childcare in your local area and these sites are listed at the back of this book. All young children attending a formal childcare setting will follow the Early Years Foundation Stage curriculum. Research childcare options early; many day nurseries have long waiting lists so it makes sense to register even if you're not sure of what your decision will be.

Talk to other parents in the area to make sure you're aware of everything available. Listen to your instincts when exploring any childcare options. The best facilities and equipment do not necessarily make for the happiest children. Will your daughter be played with and listened to?

In all childcare situations, trust and confidence in the carers are of paramount importance. In a nursery, chat to as many staff as possible and form your own impressions. When talking to a childminder, be very frank about your views and expectations to see whether you share a similar approach.

Under 5s — development stages

These are the discovery years, when your daughter is working out where she fits in the world and how much control she has over it. She is moving towards forming her own identity. Girls differ from boys in the way in which they acquire skills at this age.

- **Speech:** She is likely to be more talkative than a boy because the left hemisphere of her brain develops faster. Even before

EDUCATING

speech develops, she will enjoy looking at picture books and listening to simple stories and rhymes. Early experience of rhythm and rhyme are important to future success in reading and writing.

- **Impulse control:** She is better able to monitor and control her behaviour because her brain secretes more serotonin. Early play tends to be solitary; later she will play alongside others and eventually with them.
- **Multi-tasking:** Her occipital lobe develops faster so she has greater sensory awareness, including of others' emotions, and because it secretes more oxytocin, she has a need to nurture.

In these years it is important to show your love, give her praise, listen and chat with her. Provide plenty of opportunities for her to develop her skills and friendships, perhaps at a toddler group or nursery. By responding to her endless demands of 'pick me up', 'put me down' and 'watch me', you build her trust. By playing and reading and answering all those 'why?' questions, you develop her confidence and imagination.

Under 5s — tips for parents

- Don't obsess about her development or progress; every child is different and we've yet to see a bride in nappies!
- Admire everything she creates. Try to avoid asking, 'What's this supposed to be?' Instead, just ask her to talk about it.
- Children react very differently to being left alone. Try to be positive and calm, even if you're the one about to cry!
- Read to her and with her. Make reading an exciting and enjoyable joint activity – for example, encourage her to guess what might happen next or describe what she sees in the pictures.
- Keep open lines of communication with her carers, minders,

nanny, au pair and/or teacher. She will tell them everything, anyway!

Nursery choices — what is Montessori?

The Montessori approach is holistic and aims to develop the whole child. Fundamental to the approach is the belief that a child's early years – from birth to 6 – are the period during which they have the greatest capacity to learn.

Typically, a Montessori class has children aged between 2½ and 6 years old: the older ones help the younger ones, and this assists in social, emotional and intellectual development. Classes last for a minimum of three hours, with no fixed schedule. This enables the children to spend as much (or as little) time as they wish on any one activity. Equipment is stored around the classroom, and the children are taught that they must return one set of materials before taking another.

Frequently asked questions:
What is the difference between Montessori and traditional methods of teaching?
In Montessori schools, the child is seen as a dynamic learner, full of creative potential and in need of the maximum possible freedom to be allowed to develop as a happy, confident individual.

How is discipline dealt with in a Montessori school?
Montessori schools believe that discipline is something that should come from inside rather than being imposed by others. They do not rely on rewards and punishments. Being allowed to be free in the environment, and learning to love and care for other people, the child develops confidence and control over her own behaviour. So Montessori teachers only step in when a child's behaviour is upsetting or disruptive to others.

EDUCATING

175

How will my child fit in with a more traditional system after leaving a Montessori nursery?

Montessori children tend to be very socially comfortable. Because they have been encouraged to problem-solve and think independently, they are also happy, confident and resourceful. So they normally settle very quickly and easily into new schools. In fact, primary school teachers are often delighted to hear that your child has been in a Montessori nursery!

Ages 5–7

Your daughter is now moving out into the educational world, where she will spend much of her next eleven or more years. She will be meeting new children and adults, as well as acquiring new skills and knowledge. She will discover more and more about herself: whom she likes; what she enjoys; what she finds difficult and who she is. Your interest, support, encouragement and praise are key to the success and enjoyment of her school days. By encouraging her wider interests and activities, you can provide a richer environment within which she can explore. This involvement in her life, though in a different way than in her early years, can help you to ensure she builds her self-esteem and give her the confidence to blossom. You will learn about her expanding world as she starts to flourish in new surroundings.

5–7s – education choices

By now, your daughter will be happily settled into school and enjoying making new friends. Depending on the school she attends, she may move from an infant to a junior school when she is 7, at the end of Key Stage 1.

Wherever your daughter goes to school, she will cover the national curriculum for Key Stage 1. You can find out more about this on the website: www.direct.gov.uk. In the pre-prep departments of independent girls' schools, pupils are likely to go beyond the confines of the prescribed curriculum, including beginning to learn a modern language. They usually perform well above the national average in any assessments taken at the end of this key stage.

In these early years, your daughter may start to develop her first interests outside the classroom. Many schools will offer clubs, either during the lunch hour or after school, and it is often in Year 2 (age 6–7) that pupils first have the opportunity to learn a musical instrument. With so many options available both inside and outside school, it can be tempting to fill a child's diary with music lessons, drama clubs, swimming lessons and so on.

Your daughter may well try a new activity, only to lose interest quite quickly. Gently encourage her to persist if you think she has some aptitude but dropping one hobby may give her time to discover a new talent – it's only by trying lots of different things that she can discover what she really enjoys.

While all of these activities are both beneficial and enjoyable, remember that children also need time to play!

5–7s – development stages

These are the adventurous years, filled with school, friends and activities. Your daughter is freer at this stage than she will be for a long time. Play is her 'work', and she will become increasingly social. Her imagination flourishes, which means that she may sometimes have difficulty telling fantasy from reality.

Her fine and gross motor skills are rapidly improving. She can run and skip, colour and cut, throw a ball and ride a bike. At school she will be learning a vast range of new things: to read and write; to count and measure and to handle friendships. Her school will guide you in how best to support her learning, so ask how she is being taught to read, write, subtract, etc.

If she seems to be significantly less well coordinated than her peers, you should discuss this with your GP. Similarly, if she has difficulties learning to read, discuss your concerns with her teacher. Early diagnosis of any developmental delays or learning difficulties makes it easier to get appropriate help and support.

During these years your daughter is free to try, to take risks without worrying what others are thinking. By working through any fears, she will develop confidence, gain social skills and discover her individual personality and talents. You can help her by teaching her how to fail, as well as how to succeed. Many teenage issues, such as eating disorders and substance abuse, have roots in a fear of failure. Until she learns how to recover from failure, your daughter will believe she is only acceptable when she is successful.

At this stage her thinking is very literal and fairness is important to her. By giving her sensible and consistent boundaries, you can help to make her world safe and dependable. Implementing moral guidelines allows her to make sense of her world and her own place within it.

5–7s – tips for parents

- Keep reading with her and to her. You should both enjoy this shared activity. You can speculate on how the characters might be feeling or make up different, sometimes ridiculous, endings!
- Do label all your daughter's clothes and possessions clearly. Uniform is uniform, undies are very similar and children can get very distressed if they can't find their socks or jumper.
- If you ask her 'What did you do at school today?', she'll probably say, 'Play.' This is as it should be. Children learn through play and the curriculum is designed to enable this. Counting, weighing, listening to and telling stories are the foundations of future learning.
- School should be enjoyable. Try not to let any of your anxieties or negative past experiences spill out.
- Good parenting is about enabling your child to become her own person, and this involves trying new things, taking risks and making mistakes. After all, how did she learn to walk except by falling over?

EDUCATING

179

Thoughts from a Head — Not everyone can be Mary

At primary schools throughout the country, the nativity play is one of the major events of the school year. Despite the traditions that surround it, things have moved on considerably from the old dressing gown and frayed tea towel, charming though they were. These days you are more likely to see custom-made, designer costumes, a light and sound desk and a script that bears little resemblance to the traditional story we all knew and loved.

Finding parts for a hundred or more children takes some imagination on the part of the director. If one is to avoid a flock of eighty sheep or a host of fifty angels, it is inevitable that some more obscure characters find themselves sneaking on to the stage. The lobster in the film *Love Actually* comes to mind. Proud parents have enthusiastically applauded adventurous chickens, bad-tempered sheep and even a walking, talking jam tart!

Although every child on the stage has an important part to play, is it ever entirely possible to run a nativity in which everyone is equal? If so, one could avoid the dilemmas that inevitably surround the tricky decision as to who plays Mary. In any school this remains the dream role, the red carpet is there for only one - Mary.

Confident, articulate speakers, and even budding actresses, may be passed over for the stalwart individual who can carry out a solo without succumbing to chicken pox or tonsillitis. Perhaps even more important is that the part goes to the girl steely enough to carry the stress of such a high profile role and still be able to rejoin the lesser mortals come January, when the dizzy heights of fame come to an abrupt end. For some girls, the disappointment will be the first of its kind when they hear that they have not been 'chosen'. On top of this, they may also have to manage the disappointment of their parents, whose expectations can weigh heavily on their very young shoulders. Accepting and overcoming the feeling of being overlooked, and even that of jealousy towards the 'chosen one', is a normal emotion and a tough but important lesson we all have to face at some point in our lives.

There may, of course, be other girls desperately hoping they will not be chosen. Regardless of their parents' wishes, there are some girls for whom being Mary may prove their worst nightmare. Some will flatly refuse to play the part or have telltale tummy aches as initial rehearsals take place. However, if the casting is deftly handled, every girl will have a part they can fulfil – and enjoy – even if it means a slight jolt out of their comfort zone.

Despite its potential pitfalls and hazards, with children simultaneously tired and overexcited, the nativity play has a great deal in its favour. First and foremost, it offers girls the opportunity to gain confidence. Often parents will comment that they hardly recognise the very self-assured girl on the stage as their timid daughter. An additional advantage is that it also allows girls to learn to work as a team. They learn to take direction, begin to understand timing and have their first experiences of performing for an audience; lines have to be learnt and being ready for a cue requires patience and self-control. Recognising the talents and gifts of your fellow classmates is invaluable, and often those who may not shine in the classroom are inspired. They may be the ones who actually surprise everyone with a performance rivalling the *X Factor*! When things go wrong (which can actually be the most fun for those watching), girls are encouraged by staff to maintain poise, and this can help to develop maturity in young girls. Even reception- and nursery-aged children need to summon up a significant level of concentration as they sit still and follow the story. They are usually the ones at the front who we cannot ignore as we watch them watching with joy, excitement and lots of wriggling!

Teachers who have been providing this kind of entertainment for years know that the nativity play presents an early opportunity for a great life experience for every girl involved, as well as a tear-jerking moment for mums and dads. An enormous amount of hard work goes into presenting these shows, and for the girls, emotions can run high as the big day approaches, but the biggest benefit of any nativity play is the sheer fun it provides for the girls, staff and parents alike. Not everyone can be Mary, but there should be something for everyone.

5—7s — education Q&A

Best age to move schools

Q: We are looking to move back to the UK from abroad, mainly because of schooling. We have two girls, aged 5 and nearly 1. In that we have already missed the start of UK schooling for the eldest (currently at international pre-school), does anyone have experience of the best/easiest time to move children? I have heard the younger, the better. How difficult is it to even get into good schools unless you have applied way ahead?

A: This is a wonderful opportunity for your daughters, and the girls can only be advantaged from it. If possible, it is best to move your girls at the beginning of the academic year — in September — as this is a natural time for everyone starting the new school term. However, with such young children, you could move at any point in the next couple of years. Your youngest daughter probably won't even remember not being in the UK.

The natural transition points for changing and starting school are at 4, 7 and 11 in the British system. If you did choose to wait a couple of years, your older daughter could move into Key Stage 2 (at aged 7 rising 8) and your little one could start in early years/nursery (aged 3 rising 4). There would also be other children starting school at this point, so they wouldn't be the odd ones out.

It can be difficult to get into some so-called 'good' schools, but there are often occasional places that become available, and schools do look kindly on people moving from overseas. Do give the school as much information about your daughters' schooling as you can — especially including their school reports — and make sure you visit the school to glean as much information about it as you can. Find out also how the school integrates new pupils, as well as what they provide for new parents in terms of social events so you can also get involved in your children's school community.

Good luck with the move. It will be of benefit to the whole family.

Summer birthdays — dropping down a year

Q: *We have a 7-year-old daughter whose birthday is 31 August, and while she tries really hard at everything she is asked to do it is obvious to us as parents that she would benefit from dropping down a year. Her current prep school says they can bring her along but I feel that she will find it harder as she gets older and possibly not pass the entrance exams for senior school.*

I just wanted to get your opinion on children dropping down a year. Can they stay in that year for the duration of their education or would she have to rejoin her year group for senior school ? We have asked a local state school if they would allow her to join the year below, but they refused. But another prep school said yes. I am going round in circles with it and just want to find somewhere she is happy and working at a pace she can keep up with.

A: August birthday girls are special. Certainly, no summer or September birthday child in England or Wales can ever be 'average' on the age criterion in her year group.

Do exactly what you feel seems right for your daughter. If she seems 'young' or lacks confidence, send her to the school that will let her be in the year group where she will have all the advantages of being the oldest instead of the youngest. Indeed, were she in Northern Ireland or Scotland, she would be in that year group anyway, as their cut-off dates are earlier. There is no absolute set date, and each child should be considered as an individual. Even the youngest children who are academically fine, can be less socially mature. Small issues can make a huge difference, such as being too small or too young to engage in sports activities that others in the same year are able to do, or not being able to drive to the pub like your friends, many years down the line!

Old for the year

Take the long view. Parents of bright September birthday children rightly see that they are ready for school before their younger cohort peers and often push for acceleration into the year group where, ironically, the parents of the marginally older summer birthday children feel their daughters should be allowed NOT to be in! For both, it is worth giving your child an advantage for her whole academic career by being the oldest and most mature, rather than being the very youngest.

Check that the school can provide sufficient breadth, depth and challenge for the older child and, as long as they can, go for it.

Placing a child in a year group is a move that, once made, is hard to reverse, so starting correctly or seizing the opportunity of a change of school is important. A child over 6 usually finds it psychologically difficult to repeat a year in the same school. Once settled in the younger class, it is usually too difficult to make up the work missed if one skips a class.

Young for the year

For the very young child, consider keeping her in a good nursery for an extra year — and find a school that will support you in having done this. After all, the August birthday girl is almost a quarter of a lifetime younger than the oldest in her reception class.

Once in a year group, all independent and most maintained schools (especially given the current emphasis on personalised learning) will allow a child to stay where she is and progress through from junior to senior school with her current cohort. However, it would be wise to check the local situation. If local education authority rules prevent such progression, it is exactly the sort of case an independent school may be able to help with bursary assistance. Other parents may now be worried. 'Is my daughter in the wrong place?' If your daughter remains in the 'right' school cohort, as the majority do, don't

185

worry. If well supported at home and in school, there can be advantages in being young for the year — but that is only as long as the child is academically ranked in the top half of the year. The age and maturity disadvantage lessens as the years pass, and ability and motivation, not age, usually end up as the main factors for academic success. Girls mature sooner than boys, so the young girl may be as ready to cope as boys of average age. Above all, being the youngest can create academic challenge, which is ideal for some girls.

The very bright girl may cope well with — or even need — the academic challenge of being the youngest; a good school should be able to provide this for its oldest students as well, while you can give your daughter all the advantages that come with being developmentally mature in her year group.

Should my daughter move to a different school?

Q: My 7-year-old daughter attends an independent school and they have recommended I move her into a state school, as she is struggling with her work. Any advice, please?

A: The most important issue is whether your daughter is happy at her school. This is unlikely if she is struggling with her work; an unhappy child cannot learn. Unless your daughter can be successful at least some of the time, she won't grow into a happy, confident teenager and then she could develop more serious problems than simply academic ones.

Another important question is whether her current school is selective. If it is, the likelihood is that the pressure on her will steadily increase with each passing year. Look at what your daughter is good at. Perhaps she is artistic, musical or sporty. Try to find a school that will value her for her talents outside the classroom. Perhaps there is a less academically selective independent school in your area that would support your daughter more effectively and help her to find areas where she can succeed.

Most schools do not recommend that a child should leave unless they have very good reasons for believing that it is in the best interests of the child herself. For your daughter's sake, it is important to find a school that is better attuned to her needs and where she is able to flourish.

Ages 7–11

Your daughter should be full of excitement and delight as she continues to learn and develop, but she may also have moments of worry – how can she remember her times tables? Why won't her best friend play with her today? Has she got everything she needs for school today? Why are boys so annoying? She will also continue to ask endless questions, some of which you may not know the answer to. Finding out the answer together can be rewarding for both of you; after all, at some point she will realise that even her perfect parents do not know everything! You will still be the centre of her universe at this time, so enjoy it – it may not last throughout her teenage years. During this stage, you will be laying the foundations of a strong relationship in which two-way open communication ensures that she trusts and respects you. Establishing firm boundaries of acceptable behaviour, good manners and kindness to others will give her a frame of reference and moral standards that she will employ for ever.

7–11s – education choices

By now, your daughter will be happily enjoying school life. She will be taking on more responsibility within school and getting used to homework and a more exciting and demanding curriculum.

Depending on the school she is attending, your daughter is likely to:

- Encounter more specialist teachers, have a more formal time-table than before, have more homework and have more opportunities to join clubs and after-school activities.
- Learn to look after her belongings and to remember to have the right books and equipment at home and at school. You can help her learn to be organised by encouraging her to think about everything she needs to do each day rather than doing it for her.

- Be exposed to a dramatic increase in extracurricular options. This is a chance for her to discover new interests and talents. She may have the opportunity of representing her school in sports teams or competing in local music or drama competitions.

- Have the opportunity to join local organisations, such as Brownies, youth theatre and music ensembles. She may want to pursue her individual skills, perhaps in sport or music. Time to play is important, too, so make sure your daughter's schedule also gives her time to relax!

- Be preparing to take her Key Stage 2 tests at the end of Year 6 (at some schools). The results of these tests may be used by her secondary school to help them assess her academic ability upon entering the school. Many independent schools do not do Key Stage testing, and many independent secondary schools do not use these test results in any part of their admissions process. However, if your daughter is taking Key Stage 2 tests, you will want to help her prepare and do her best.

Choosing a secondary school

You will be starting to think about which is the best secondary school for your daughter. Choosing the right school can seem a daunting and stressful task. Here are some factors you may want to consider to help you make this decision.

Location

Be realistic about how your daughter will get to and from school. Remember that she will have after-school or weekend activities, including matches, drama rehearsals and music evenings. You will also want to attend many of these activities, so don't underestimate the additional burden that a long journey may entail for all of you.

EDUCATING

Academic standards

Remember that exam league tables are only one measure of a school's success. You will want your daughter's education to be more than just her exam results. Find out where leavers go to continue their education. Do they reach their first choice of destination? What does the school say about its 'value added'? This is a measure of pupils' final achievements compared to what might have been expected, based on their attainment when they joined the school.

Size of school and class size

The size of a school can have a big impact on how a child feels about the experience of school itself. Will your daughter thrive in a large, bustling environment or would the oppor-tunity to be a bigger fish in a smaller pond suit her better? Check average class sizes, too. Smaller classes generally mean greater teacher input per pupil.

Single-sex or co-ed

Again, this isn't necessarily an either/or question, as there will be schools that are co-educational for some age groups but offer single-sex teaching for others. Single-sex schools offer many advan-tages for both boys and girls. Visit www.MyDaughter.co.uk for infomation about girls' schools. You know your daughter; consider in which environment she is most likely to thrive and be happy.

Independent or state?

Find out about all the secondary schools in your area. Don't assume that fee-paying schools are beyond your means. Many offer means-tested bursaries and/or scholarships. If you live in an area where the best and most popular state schools are oversubscribed, find out about their admissions criteria well in advance, as well as what options exist if you don't get your preferred choice.

School facilities

Don't get seduced by state-of-the-art facilities. The ethos and 'feel' of a school are more important than buildings, and excellent teaching and learning can take place in very modest surroundings.

Changing at 11 or 13?

The majority of girls will move to their senior school at 11. However, some maintained schools operate a middle-school system with transfer at 13, and some independent prep schools continue to 13 with senior schools beginning in Year 9. If this is an option in your area, think about it carefully. Some pupils may benefit from the extra two years of being the oldest in their school between the ages of 11 and 13. On the other hand, girls tend to be more mature and are often ready to move on at 11. This decision may well depend on your geographical location and your daughter's school.

All-through schools

Some schools will take pupils right through from the age of 2 or 3 to 18. This can give fantastic continuity of educational provision and the formation of important long-lasting friend-ships – for parents as well as for pupils!

Day or boarding?

Again, this is not necessarily an either/or question. Many boarding schools offer weekly or flexi-boarding, which can be an ideal solution for busy families in which both parents work. Families whose work may cause them to relocate often choose boarding schools so that their children's education is not inter-rupted at a crucial time. It's not only independent schools that offer boarding, either. For information on state boarding schools, go to www.sbsa.org.uk, and for more general information about the benefits of boarding, see www.boarding.org.uk.

EDUCATING

Special needs

If your child has additional learning needs, requires support or is particularly gifted, you will want to know that the school you choose will provide the right environment and resources for her to thrive. When you visit the school, ask to meet the special needs coordinator as well as the Head to discuss these issues fully.

Faith schools

Faith schools have received a great deal of publicity, both positive and negative. Critics argue that they are exclusive and do not promote religious tolerance. Supporters argue the opposite – that pupils learn about other faiths and that such schools often have dedicated teachers, a caring and supportive ethos and excellent results. Visit and talk to people – and make your own decision.

7–11s – development stages

Your daughter is still in the adventurous phase; she is not yet full of the self-consciousness that will affect her teenage years. Her thinking is still fairly concrete: she is concerned about right and wrong, good and bad. Her world is expanding, and a wider range of adults and children will begin to influence her. She is becoming capable of more abstract reasoning and will ask lots of questions, looking to you for answers. In these years you have the opportunity to help her to work through her fears, develop confidence, gain social skills and discover her own individual personality. By maintaining reasonable and consistent boundaries, you can support and guide her while giving her rules for life. She may lie ('I didn't do it'), steal ('I was just borrowing it') and whine ('Why can't I?'), and your responses will shape her. By teaching her about manners and responsibilities, you are laying the foundations for the well-grounded adult she will grow into.

It is important that she has time to follow her personal interests and to develop her creativity. Her interests may become lifelong pursuits. Involve her in choices; she needs to develop resourcefulness, independence and self-assurance.

This is the age at which most parents choose to talk to their daughters about sex. There is a wide range of resources to help you in this difficult discussion. She will be hearing what her friends think they 'know', so instead you can ensure that she learns from you, her most trusted adviser. Read more on this topic on p 49, What should I be telling my daughter about sex, and when?

7–11s — tips for parents

- School should continue to be a place where she has fun as she learns. Lots of praise and encouragement from you will help to deepen confidence in her abilities. Support her learning and encourage her to enjoy all the different activities that school offers. Join her in outside activities that complement school and help her to discover different skills and social groups.
- Help her to develop good study habits. Provide a quiet place to do homework; look through her work, offering praise and encouragement and asking questions; help by testing spellings, times tables, etc. and support her when she is asked to do research.
- Encourage her to have a wide circle of friends rather than just one or two 'best friends', as this spreads the emotional load so that when the occasional but inevitable fall-outs occur, she has back-up.
- If she becomes reluctant to go to school, look for a pattern: does she have a spelling test or PE on Wednesdays? A different

EDUCATING

193

teacher? How are her friendships? Girls' friendships are the most important things in their lives at every age, so this is an important aspect to keep a close eye on.

• Try not to get directly involved in your daughter's inevitable friendship tangles. Parent to parent discussions seldom solve, and usually even inflame, the issue. Talk with her about how she could handle the current situation. She will need to develop her own skills to resolve her problems; you cannot and should not do everything. Approach her teacher if it's causing her real distress.

Smoothing the move to a new school

Your daughter's new school has been settled upon, and soon she will be heading off for her first day. How can you help it to go as smoothly as possible?

Take any opportunity for her to visit the school in advance. Most schools have some kind of induction day for new pupils. If not, ask if she can be shown round again – just a brief tour to refresh your memories. Look out for public events at the school and go along. It will help your daughter feel part of the school and help to familiarise her with her new surroundings. If your daughter doesn't know anyone else at this school, ask the school to put you in touch with someone. It will be a useful contact for you as well as for her.

If the school is in a new area, drive past a few times. Get out a map and show her where the school is in relation to home and to other familiar places. If your daughter is going to be travelling independently or by school coach, do the journey there and back several times, showing her what to look out for just before she gets to school and as she leaves school at the end of the day.

Talk to your daughter about how she's feeling about the move.

Be prepared for a mixture of emotions, most likely both excitement and apprehension. Talk with her about previous experiences of change – both hers and yours – and share your experiences and how you felt and reassure her that change is always a time of mixed emotions.

Leave the school's prospectus lying around along with any newsletters they've sent you so that she can quietly look through them whenever she wants to. Check the information that the school has given you about arrangements for the start of term and make sure your daughter knows what the school has planned for the first day and what she needs to take with her. If the school has asked for uniform and personal possessions to be named, make sure that's done in advance. They are likely to be checked in the first day or so, and new girls hate to be seen as having failed to conform.

Make sure your daughter knows how to contact you in case of an emergency. Programme your contact details into her mobile – as well as those of another friend or family member she can contact if you're not available. If she doesn't have a mobile, write the numbers on a piece of card and let her put that, and some money for an emergency phone call, in a safe place so she knows where to find it. (You'd be amazed how reassuring that can be.)

On the day . . . Make sure she gets to school in good time. Wish her good luck and smile – at least until you're out of sight!

Moving to secondary school — girls' worries

The move from primary to secondary school is both an exciting and daunting prospect: exciting for all the new opportunities and experiences it promises; daunting for exactly the same reason!

The formative experience of visiting new, prospective schools

EDUCATING

195

and meeting new students and teachers brings about a massive expansion in young people's horizons and offers unimaginable possibilities to young minds. During this process, issues bob to the surface of young people's consciousness that can underpin their security and happiness. Be prepared for this. Many 10 and 11-year-olds share the same worries:

- what are the lunches like?
- how much homework is there?
- what if I get lost?

It would be easy to dismiss these as trivial, especially since these particular worries tend to evaporate after a day or two in senior school. But at the point at which these concerns are often voiced (usually six to twelve months before a child starts), they are real and pressing concerns.

School lunches

Some junior school children have had the experience of packed lunches and may have opted for them because they already have a fear of trying food that is not familiar. This is understandable, as 10 and 11-year-olds are still developing their 'palate', and this may make them fearful of unfamiliar flavours and textures. But at the same time, one aspect of school is to foster healthy eating habits and confident encounters with new experiences. If you have a girl with this particular worry, tell her that most school lunches are organised to ensure that everyone has the option of a good, hot lunch in the middle of a busy and tiring day (remember, a senior school day with extracurricular activities may go until 6 pm – significantly longer than a junior school day, which may end at 3.15 pm). Many schools have three hot options a day, including a vegetarian option and pasta, as well as a salad bar. If you are able to, ask if you can see a copy of a sample menu, so that she can see some of the available options. If the chosen school has a tuck shop, it may be worth telling her about this, as well as any little facts you can ascertain, such as any effort the catering staff go to to provide fun days like wiggly worms (spaghetti) on Halloween and pink custard on Valentine's Day. Hopefully, such anecdotes can help to diminish her fears and even have her look forward to such events.

One challenge that remains for senior schools is the transition from tight junior school controls over 'snacks' to a freer experience in which children make more of their own decisions. A healthy tuck shop is important, but most do not ban chocolate and crisps. Instead, secondary school children are taught the need for balance and moderation and informed choices.

Homework

Children in junior schools have widely ranging experiences of homework. For some, it means the loose and unstructured experience of 'a project'; for others, it is irregular and inconsistent. For some it may be a nightly torture of work to be delivered each morning without fail. Whatever the Year 6 experience, many children expect that it will be much worse at senior school. At the same time, those pupils who have been bored in Year 6 may look forward to this challenge.

Homework is about either going over (reinforcing) what the pupils have learnt during the lesson or working independently to discover something new. It is important that the girls know that there can be flexibility if they really cannot do a homework assignment, and for some students, even being told that their parent can write a note in their book or in their planner to this effect reassures them. It is important that pupils, and especially those new to secondary school, are organised enough to do their homework when it is set and to try their best. But most teachers don't expect their young charges to be superhuman and will always listen if they have had a problem.

A tip for new senior school parents is to keep an eye on the amount of other evening activities children have during the week once they start senior school. Parents need to support the school's expectations of homework; if they don't, it is their child who will suffer.

Getting lost

After seven years in first and middle schools, where they know the site intimately, many Year 6 children worry about how they will learn their way around a new site – especially as they realise that they will be required to move around to different lessons. In junior school most lessons are held in the same classroom, but in senior school, children regularly move around the site to different rooms four or five times a day. This makes the children's concern about getting lost quite normal. How does one find one's way around a new and much bigger site with strange buildings and room numbers that may not appear logical?

The answer is that it is a natural concern, one that most new Year 7s will experience (not to mention new teachers); they will, of course, receive a map and they will most likely be given several opportunities to practise finding their way around. In the first weeks of the autumn term, teachers are often asked to let students out of lessons early so they can find their way to the next one! And these teachers are also asked to be patient and understanding when new pupils arrive late. In this way, while most 11-year-olds worry that they will not find their way around, they all do – it just takes practice. In fact, within a few days of being at senior school, new pupils will know lots of different routes around the school buildings, including all the secret nooks and crannies and shortcuts!

Can boredom be a good thing? The pros and cons of clubs and activities

Should I be organising more for my daughter? Will she miss out if I don't? These questions will cross the minds of all parents at some point – or several points – during their daughters' lives. When we are surrounded by a host of opportunities for out-of school clubs, classes and holiday activities, it can be difficult not to feel under pressure to sign our daughters up for everything available. But how do we decide what is right?

The best advice is to start with your daughter and ask yourself (and, of course, her) if she has a particular interest that is not being properly developed at present. Perhaps she loves to dance or act, and she doesn't have the chance to do this at school, or perhaps she is fascinated by craft and wants to spend more time doing this. If so, this is a good reason to explore additional opportunities in the evenings, or at weekends or during the holidays. In addition to enabling your daughter to pursue her passion, such activities can be very rewarding for both parent and child.

Another good reason to look at out-of-school clubs and activities is to provide an opportunity for your daughter to mix socially, either deepening existing friendships by sharing other activities, or by establishing new friendship groups. Holiday camps or summer schools can be a good way to stave off the boredom of a long holiday when other friends are away. However, a note of caution here: don't try to make your daughter develop new friends. While very young children can often play quite happily with complete strangers, older girls become – quite rightly – much more discriminating in their choice of playmate, and these relationships cannot be forced.

Children need space and time to create their own entertainment – a little boredom is a marvellous thing, as it allows the development of creative thinking and a wonderful imagination.

Over-organisation is almost invariably counter-productive; if you are rushing your daughter from class to club to team practice, then she will have little time to think, let alone grow and mature as an independent thinker. As she grows older, you want her to become less dependent on you, rather than more, and if you are effectively controlling what she does and when, then this will not be allowed to happen.

In a similar vein, as parents we can feel that our daughters should attend clubs and classes because it is 'good for them', or because we fear that they will be left behind if they don't. If Mandarin lessons are all the rage, for instance, then you may feel that you are damaging your daughter's life chances if you do not enrol her immediately. The truth of the matter is that your daughter has a lifetime to learn any practical skills she may need. The most important factor of all is that when she becomes an adult, she is as well balanced emotionally and socially as an 18-year-old can expect to be. She can learn Mandarin at any time on a crash course during her university years or later. If, however, she is carrying with her into adult-hood the resentment of having been made to spend time learning a language when all she wanted to do was play, this may hold her back further.

Essentially, choosing out-of-school activities is all about balance. Your daughter should not feel overtired, overstressed or overstretched – if she does, cut back on what she is doing immediately! Look at the bigger picture of your daughter's life – she has years ahead of her to do all sorts of activities. She doesn't need to do everything today, and ultimately she will be happier for just learning how to 'be', rather than always how to 'do'.

7–11s — education Q&A

Q: Please could you give me some book titles to help my daughter, as she is aged 9 rising 10 and dyslexic?

A: Many dyslexic girls aged 9–10 have their confidence rocked when they see their peers begin to race ahead, and it can feel all too easy for them to give up on a task that seems impossible. When confronted with a situation like this, the Toe by Toe reading scheme (see www.toe-by-toe.co.uk) can be a great help. This is a day-to-day scheme that involves a parent sitting with their daughter for ten minutes. It is well structured and starts at the very beginning with phonetic sounds and carries on right through until adult reading ability. Because it is an ongoing process involving repeating each sound, it works by moving the knowledge of the phonetic sounds into the long-term memory. And because it involves the two of you together, it is fun and can achieve excellent results. For more information on specific book titles for your daughter, read the 'Ideas for reluctant readers' on p 250.

11+ hopes and fears

Q: My daughter is doing her 11+ in one week. Her teacher, tutor and I all know she can pass this exam. She is very bright but she seems to have lost all motivation along with confidence in herself. She has become very quiet and despondent. Her results have been slipping, and I would love to know what to do to put back a little of her spark and hunger to succeed, as she used to love doing well at school. Any suggestions?

A: If both your daughter's teacher and tutor have confidence in her ability, then she is clearly a bright girl, but even bright girls can suffer from sudden doubts, loss of confidence and all-round 'wobbles'. This is probably the first significant challenge she has faced, and it is only natural that she is feeling fearful. Rather than trying to 'put back a little of her spark and hunger to succeed', perhaps try focusing on reassuring her of your unconditional love for her — in particular, for the person she is rather than for her academic success. She may be worrying about the future in a general way, fearing the inevitable changes ahead, or she may be frightened that she will let you and her teachers down. In either case, by reminding her of your confidence in her as a whole person and your excitement about what the future holds, she should begin to regain her spark.

Does my daughter need a tutor?

Q: My daughter is in Year 5 at our local primary school and is doing really well. I would like to put her in for entrance tests for some private senior schools next year, as I think she would really benefit from the opportunities and facilities on offer there. However, everyone I speak to tells me she won't stand a chance unless she is tutored for the tests from now onwards, as she hasn't covered the curriculum. I always promised myself I wouldn't get sucked into this kind of competitive parenting and playground gossip, but I don't want my daughter to miss out because I didn't give her the right chances. Is a tutor necessary in this situation?

A 1: In the run-up to entrance tests for schools, parents can — very understandably — become anxious, and some indeed opt for tutoring because everyone else seems to be doing it and they want to give their daughter the same preparation. Most 11+ entrance tests do not require special knowledge or unusual skills — however, ask the schools for details or past papers to check. On the face of it, as your daughter is doing really well, tutoring would seem unnecessary. It may be that all you need to do is buy some practice test booklets and ask her to try out stories and maths problems under your supervision. However, if you feel she has gaps in her understanding, or lacks confidence, you might consider a little extra tutoring as a 'booster'. If you really feel that without substantial tutoring she won't get in, then perhaps you should consider whether she would manage with the pace once there, or whether there is a danger her confidence will be damaged and she will not thrive.

A 2: Parents are keen to see their child do well in forthcoming examinations and so are sometimes persuaded that she needs the top-up that a private tutor can provide. Resorting to tutoring does not always imply dissatisfaction with the teaching at school; some one-on-one sessions can demystify those parts of the syllabus that are proving problematic. The individual attention and tailored practice a tutor will give can do wonders for a child's confidence and help to improve examination technique. But before you put 'private tutor' into Google, here are three points worth considering:

- Go for word-of-mouth recommendations and check to see if the tutor has had a CRB check (Criminal Records Bureau).
- If possible, tell the school that you feel extra help is needed: your child may not be giving you the full story of her shortcomings and the school may be putting on clinics and helplines already.
- While tutoring can provide a boost that justifies the investment, there is little point in preparing your daughter successfully for an exam to enter a selective school if she flounders once she is there. A good tutor, like a good school, should foster independence and not dependence.

Ages 11–16

As she goes through puberty, your daughter will present you with some 'interesting' dilemmas: how much independence and freedom should you give her? Why does she act like a child one minute and an adult the next? Which GCSEs should she choose? At times she may seem to reject your opinions and values as she measures them against those of her friends. Academic pressures will build as she works towards taking public exams, and social pressures will dominate her thinking and affect her behaviour. By helping her to appreciate that success comes in many forms, that how you look is only a small part of who you are, by gradually extending the boundaries you established when she was younger and, above all, by praising, encouraging and appreciating her, you will enable her to become her own, special self.

11–16s – education choices

The majority of girls will make a move at the age of 11, either to a new school or to the senior department of their existing school. In some cases they will transfer to senior school from a preparatory school or middle school at the age of 13.

In either situation, they will find themselves studying:
- a broader range of subjects, including, perhaps, additional modern languages or Latin
- a broader range of technology and creative subjects
- more specialist teaching in science

Your daughter will have more homework and she should enjoy more extracurricular activities. She may join a variety of clubs, music ensembles or training squads for particular sports.

Years 7 to 9 (Key Stage 3)

This is a time when your daughter is likely to develop interests and enthusiasms in particular subjects and she may start to think about careers. Her first big decisions will come at the age of 13–14 in Year 9, when she chooses the subjects she will study at GCSE level. Some schools seem to encourage pupils to take as many GCSEs as possible, but in reality universities and employers are generally looking for quality rather than quantity. So it may be better for your daughter to focus on getting eight excellent grades than twelve slightly lower ones.

When helping her to choose her GCSE options, encourage your daughter to think carefully about her ambitions, interests and abilities rather than about which subjects her best friend is choosing. The two of you should talk to her teachers about where her talents lie and what grades she might realistically aim for. At this stage it is vital that she doesn't close any doors and opts for a broad, balanced range of subjects. While she may take some subjects at A level without having studied them previously, others require her to have a good grade GCSE in the same subject.

At this time she should also think about how she learns best: does she prefer essay-writing to practical subjects? Would modular courses, for which there are exams after each chunk of a syllabus, suit her better than exams at the end of the two-year course? There is advice on helping your 11–14-year-old to learn the best approach on www.direct.gov.uk/en/Parents/Schoolslearninganddevelopment.

Years 10 and 11 (Key Stage 4)

Years 10 and 11 will be busy for your daughter, as she studies her chosen General Certificate of Secondary Education (GCSE) courses. In many independent schools, some of her examination courses will follow the International GCSE syllabus (IGCSE). The decision to opt for IGCSE has been controversial, as it is not universally recognised by the government for league table purposes. However, it is perceived by many experienced teachers as the more rigorous and demanding course than the GCSE and is believed to ensure much better preparation for A levels and higher education.

Some GCSE courses are now modular, with examinations at regular intervals throughout the two-year course. Your daughter will need to hit the ground running and work consistently to develop good study skills, rather than just having a race to revise for the final exams. Try to encourage her to plan her time and keep up to date with projects and assignments to avoid any last-minute panics.

If your daughter's school ends at age 16, or if she will be moving to a different sixth form, it is worth beginning to consider this process in earnest in Year 10. Year 11 will be very busy with exams and coursework, so it's worth taking the time to review the options early on. Many girls in a single-sex school until GCSE think that a move to a co-educational environment for sixth form will be the best preparation for university life and beyond. This may be true for some girls, but think very carefully before moving your daughter from an environment in which she is known, settled, happy and doing well. Many sixth form courses are also modular, and it can take a while to get used to a new environment, meaning the results of early modules may suffer if students move schools.

When considering sixth form provision, there are additional options to consider other than just A levels. A growing number of schools offer the International Baccalaureate (IB), while others are building extended projects into their curriculum or the new Pre-U qualification. Sixth form prospectuses from individual institutions will give you further details on each school's approach, but in the meantime there are useful websites listed in the back of this book.

The examination structure in Scotland is somewhat different. Please see the Parents' guide – Scottish qualifications (p265) for further information.

11–16s — development stages

This is the 'me' stage – her narcissistic years. Your daughter's world revolves around herself. Her thoughts are full of what people think of her and how she looks. She is becoming her own person, developing her own opinions and tastes. In the process of separating from you, she will often take up the voices of her peers before she finds her own. Puberty wreaks havoc on your daughter's brain as well as, often, on the peace of your home. You can feel rejected and worried by her moodiness and contrariness.

The prefrontal cortex of a girl's brain is undergoing significant change, as the synapses (connections) begin a period of rapid growth. During these years a teenager's ability to empathise with or to distinguish emotions in others declines. Hormones surge through her brain and will affect virtually everything in her life. She is trying to establish who she is as separate from you, as well as to find some independence and control. However, as your daughter goes through puberty, she will need your advice and understanding. For instance, when she starts her periods – particularly if this is earlier or later than her friends – she will want your practical and emotional support. She may be dissatisfied with her newly emerging curves, and your reassurance will help her become a confident young woman.

Although she will often be awkward and unsure of herself, she will need freedom to become independent. However, boundaries remain very important. She needs time to herself and time with her peers. Her friendships are central to her life and happiness at this time. Your daughter knows she has your love, but she needs close friends to help her to grow. She will probably want a boyfriend, and you should negotiate acceptable rules about where and when she can see him. Open communication is very important; explain any concerns you have so she knows that your rules are because you care about her, not because you are trying to restrict her.

EDUCATING

Your daughter's peers are extremely important to her, and she may seem to value their opinions above yours. This is where the values and rules you helped to instil earlier will provide a yardstick for her. She may test your boundaries, but if you can keep your self-control while you negotiate with her, she will be able to learn useful skills for her future.

Girls are fascinated by relationships. Paradoxically, she may wish to express her individuality by slavishly following fashion and seeking peer group approval. But don't be fooled – beneath a veneer of sophistication, your teenage daughter may feel very insecure and will still have a continuing need for approval.

11–16s – tips for parents

- Keep doing all the things mentioned in the 7–11 stage!
- By now, she should be doing her homework away from distractions, in a space of her own. She will probably tell you that playing music helps her to concentrate – and it might be true! Continue to encourage her to discuss her work with you; give plenty of praise and ask loads of questions.
- Make sure you know her friends' names; they are very important to her and to her happiness. Don't offer opinions on them unless asked. She will learn about herself by sampling a range of friends, some of whom you may not be comfortable with. The most important thing is to keep your lines of communication open and if you try to direct or control her friendships, she may begin to shut you out.
- Don't try to be your daughter's best friend. She should have lots of friends, but she only has one mother. Aim to be the best mother you can be. This includes setting and holding boundaries. Children feel secure when they know there are limits. No matter how hard she pushes, she won't stop loving you just because you say no. In fact, she will feel

safer and better loved, however much she huffs and slams doors!

- When she is choosing her GCSE subjects, listen to her, get her to talk to her teachers and offer your opinion, but remember that she is the one who will be studying these subjects, not you.

- Form realistic expectations of her academic potential by talking to her teachers. Remember that academic success is only one way of succeeding. Many 'successful' members of society did not shine at school. Resourcefulness, creativity and perseverance, for example, are key qualities that are not directly measured by our academic system.

- The best way of protecting your daughter against the perils of eating disorders and substance abuse is to help her to build self-esteem. Value her for who she is rather than for what she does. Help her to see that there are more important things than appearance, possessions and clothes. Give her values that will sustain her through difficult times.

Thoughts from a Head — letter-writing in a digital world

Parents today may bemoan the fact that their children no longer pay attention to neat handwriting and accuracy of punctuation, spelling and grammar in their day-to-day communication. However, while still being able to empathise with and understand our children, we also need to accept that the world they live in requires different skills from those we needed when we grew up.

We need to be mindful that the world our teenagers inhabit has changed significantly, and there are differences that we should also not underestimate. Letter-writing, including thank-you notes, were a common feature of the

EDUCATING

childhood of many of today's parents. It is still common among people (mainly women, truth be told) of this generation to send hand-written thank-you notes for a variety of reasons. But this is one of the traditions that may not survive the development of technology; today, day-to-day communication takes a different form.

Now, if our children wish to communicate, they will use text, email, instant messaging and Facebook to do so. Handwriting becomes irrelevant. In these forms, punctuation, spelling and grammar may be utilitarian and only used for sense, rather than obeying any pre-set rules. Young people are still taught these rules, and they do know the importance of following them in certain contexts — for example, in GCSE coursework, in an examination, writing a formal report. The skills are still there but, in children's everyday contact with each other, shortcuts apply and, as long as they can be understood by their audience, the formal language conventions are not of great concern.

Texting at speed and making yourself understood using a particular code is a skill of its own. It may not be a skill shared by all of their parents' generation. Other skills — writing a long, entertaining and reflective letter to a friend or keeping a diary (which, again, encourages you to process and reflect on your experiences) as opposed to an online blog — these may die out. But the world our children live in and the future we are preparing them for is not the same as the one in which we grew up. Empathise with your children - but also recognise the differences in these worlds, and appreciate the different skill set our children may require as a result.

11—16s — education Q&A

Q: How do I help my daughter to settle into her new senior school and to cope with the pressures that come with it?

A 1: Starting senior school is the beginning of a new life stage for your daughter. As with all life stages, attitude and approach matter. The most important thing you can do is to be overwhelmingly positive and excited for your daughter, and to say how proud you are that she is moving up. This will give her a boost that helps her to deal with any anxiety; it will help make her more relaxed, and if she is more relaxed, she will automatically find it easier to make friends. Encourage her to throw herself into everything; say that this is a real opportunity for her to do all sorts of things, and that she will really enjoy the variety. Whether she is at boarding or day school, talk to her every evening if you can, to ask her what she is doing, and to give wise, upbeat advice if she seems slightly wobbly. Remember that the focus is on her, not you — if at all possible, avoid saying that you are missing her or that things will never quite be the same again. Look forward with enthusiasm, ensuring you don't look backward, and she will take your lead.

A 2: When asked to summarise how they felt after their first week at school, a group of new senior school girls chose these words: tired, excited, ecstatic, busy, comfortable, at home, rushed, challenged, happy, pleased . . . These words go some way towards describing the kaleidoscope of new feelings that the girls are experiencing at this stage.

One thing is certain — your daughter will be busy. Busy meeting lots of new people, forming new relationships with staff and other girls, organising bags and lockers, handing in homework on the right day and at the right time, giving in reply slips and forms, getting to registration twice a day, assembly, lessons, break times, lunchtime activities and getting ready to catch the bus home. She will have had to absorb an astounding volume of new information during these first few weeks, and she may be emotionally and physically exhausted, but this will quickly ease as she builds up the stamina and confidence to enjoy her new environment.

Naturally, it will take some girls longer to settle in than others. This can be due to various factors: travelling new longer distances to school, perhaps for the first time by bus or on her own, or leaving the familiarity of a small junior school and junior school friends.

What can you do to help?

Encourage your daughter to participate in as many clubs and activities at school as possible and to enquire about the possibility of initiating new clubs and activities if she has a specific interest that is not met. This is a great way to meet new friends with similar interests.

Your daughter will be tired, so encourage early nights and getting as much rest at weekends as possible.

If she will let you, help with the practical matters of being organised during these early days. Post a copy of her school and homework timetables up at home — this could be helpful both for homework assignments and for determining which books and equipment need to be taken in to school each day.

Packing the school bag the previous night is often more productive than doing it in the morning, and a whiteboard in the bedroom or kitchen can be a useful way of reminding girls what needs to packed.

Find out about the support network available to your daughter — subject teachers, form tutors, Head of Year, peer mentors, school nurse and so on. If you have queries or concerns, do get in touch with the school — they will be keen to help.

Sixth form choices — A levels or IB?

Q: Can you point me in the right direction for deciding whether IB or A levels are the right choice for my daughter?

A: There are some key differences between the A level and the IB diploma qualifications, although both lead equally well into higher education.

The IB diploma requires students to take six subjects (three at higher level and three at standard level) for the full two years of sixth form study, giving students a broad academic profile and allowing their skills to develop over an extended period of time. There are no public examinations at the end of the lower sixth year.

In contrast to this, A level courses generally allow a narrower focus of academic study and students are usually examined at the end of both the lower and upper sixth years. Students taking the A level pathway may therefore need to adjust quickly to their new courses in readiness for their AS examinations. Some schools, however, opt for a linear approach to A levels, either by offering the Pre-U course or simply choosing to enter students for all their module examinations at the end of the upper sixth, rather than taking some of these examinations at the end of the lower sixth. Most new A level courses also have either a reduced amount or no coursework, which means that the bulk of the assessment lies in examinations alone.

IB courses are designed to let the student develop their knowledge base and their critical abilities over a longer period, giving a chance for the student to mature before they are formally assessed. In addition, all IB courses have an element of coursework, which reduces the load on a student during final examinations. The IB diploma also requires the student to complete an extended essay, a course in the Theory of Knowledge (TOK) and a range of creativity, action and service (CAS), alongside their individual subjects. This core of work is a vital element in the IB diploma and universities have shown a particular interest in both the extended essay and the TOK components.

Alongside their key subjects, A level students may also be offered the new extended project, a research assignment similar to the IB's extended essay.

Helping your daughter to choose

Before choosing between these two pathways, your daughter should not only consider which subjects she most enjoys and where her strengths lie, but also how she learns. Personal qualities, such as being well organised, are also important considerations.

The decision about which course to follow must focus on one simple question: 'What is the right course for me, given my interests, work habits and ability?' It is vital to consider all aspects of each approach alongside one's own personal strengths and interests.

Q: Why can't my daughter take ten GCSEs?

A: It is important that each girl takes the selection and number of GCSEs that is appropriate for her. We understand that very bright girls want to continue with all their spread of subjects, including three separate sciences, two modern foreign languages, Latin and possibly two if not three of religious studies, geography and history. Unfortunately, this number of GCSE subjects is usually not possible, nor advisable.

Firstly, most schools' timetables do not allow for more than eight or nine GCSE options, as schedules must also allow for the 'extras', such as Personal, Social and Health Education, careers, PE and RE.

Secondly, most schools would prefer that their pupils gained eight good results than ten mediocre ones, particularly as most universities do not want or require an applicant to have a great number of GCSE subjects. Also be aware that as the competition 'heats up' for university places, having eight A and A* grades is much better than having ten grades with a B included.

Thirdly — and this is becoming ever more apparent — new GCSE courses require students to undertake assessments throughout the two-year course. Controlled assessments, investigative skills assignments, coursework and modular examinations are the norm under the new specifications and even the brightest and most dedicated students are finding it hard to manage their workload, when they also want to continue with their sport, music, drama or outdoor pursuits.

The pursuit of perfection

Q: My 13-year-old daughter is showing increased anxiety about writing. She prefers to do all her work on the computer, allowing her to repeat it continuously until it is perfect. Any mistakes she makes in her written books she finds hard to deal with and wants to start a new exercise book. This is becoming worse, to the point where she does not really want to write at all and all homework is taking a ridiculous amount of time to complete.

A: There appear to be two separate but very closely linked issues here. One is the desire for perfection and not being able to 'let go of' or stop a piece of work because it may not be perfect, and the other is relying on the computer as a kind of safety blanket, due to the invisibility of crossing-out or correction. Both are signs or symptoms of the onset of an obsessive disorder, which, if left untreated, may develop into a more serious obsessive-compulsive disorder. It is important to seek professional help now. A good course of action would probably be to speak to her GP about a recommended counsellor.

As a parent, you also need to work closely with your daughter's school to set up a system in which your daughter only spends the allotted time on her homework and then stops. She should also be encouraged to put herself in situations where she takes risks and has to manage without being perfect. How does she react in other situations – for example, to messiness, baking or cooking or getting involved in outdoor activities? How does she respond to timed tests in class or at examination times? Is she managing to complete these? Is the school allowing her to work on a computer during class, or is she happy to take rough notes longhand?

Going forward, your daughter needs to feel more confidence in being able to write things down herself, to stop being fixed on using a computer and to feel comfortable with work that may not be perfect. Rest assured your daughter is not alone in this. There are many girls who refuse to hand in work that they think is not perfect and take far too long on it. Professional counselling has helped a number of these girls to learn coping skills. Do seek help now, as this will allow your daughter to make good progress before GCSE examinations and coursework start to have an impact.

My daughter is so disorganised!

Q: My 12-year-old daughter is very bright but also very disorganised, and this is leading to all sorts of problems at school. Either she forgets to do homework, or does it and forgets to hand it in and then loses it. She loses books, PE kit, uniforms, keys, phones, etc. on a regular basis. These are usually found again later, but not always. She is always asked to pay for replacements. Consequently, she is frequently given punishments at school, including detentions. Her teachers are very frustrated by this, as it gets in the way of what she could be capable of. I was exactly the same as a child, but I got so frustrated with myself around her age that I made huge efforts and am now renowned as incredibly organised. I have tried to help her to set up systems, but nothing works for more than a few days and I think she needs to find her own system. I'm sure she's not the only one in her age group, but I am very concerned that unless she sorts it out, she will severely limit her own capabilities. Please can you offer any suggestions?

A: You are quite right: this needs to be addressed if your daughter is to make the most of the opportunities available to her at school and beyond. If you are worried that her disorganisation might be a sign of a learning disability, then consider arranging an assessment by an educational psychologist — often the brightest pupils have particular learning needs that an expert can help to identify.

In the meantime, helping to give her the tools to organise herself starts with aiding her to set up systems. What you do in this respect is really important, and you should not give up, as consistency and repetition are the real keys to success. A written checklist that she carries around may help, but only as long as your daughter feels the desire to follow it; if she is not motivated to change, or would prefer not to recognise her disorganisation as an issue (and, being bright, this is entirely possible), then you may need to adopt other approaches. These might include spending a few minutes every evening writing out a schedule with her for

EDUCATING

217

the following day and then running through this in the morning. The more regular you can make your home life, the better — homework at exactly the same time each evening, for instance — as this creates a really strong structure, which your daughter can learn to internalise and apply to other aspects of her life. To help her at school, you need to draw as many of her teachers into this organising process as possible, to act as a strong support. A routine whereby she is reminded by every teacher of a certain set of phrases — for example, 'bag, book, phone, keys' — before she leaves a classroom or an activity could be of enormous use, especially if you use exactly the same phrases at home and when she is out and about. It is always far better to reward than to punish, and setting up a system whereby she gains points if, for example, she arrives back home with all her equipment, could also help. Essentially, the most important piece of advice is not to give up; it will be worth it.

How do I make her practise the violin!

Q: My daughter is 12 and has been playing the violin for over three years. She appears to enjoy the concerts and orchestra events she is involved in and has done reasonably well in her grade exams, but I am finding it increasingly difficult to persuade her to practise. I realise she has other claims on her time now, but I think she will really regret it if she gives up at this stage. How hard should I push her to practise and keep going with this?

A: This is such a common problem for young musicians, as they understandably lose heart when they try hard to take their playing to a new, higher level. Unnecessary, excess pressure from parents at this stage could prove counterproductive in the long term.

While musically you may feel that your daughter is at a temporary standstill, please don't underestimate the important enrichment your daughter is experiencing while playing in orchestras and concerts. Playing in such groups offers a young musician the opportunity to develop those much needed life skills such as social interaction, communication and teamwork. Like playing in sports teams, playing in orchestras and singing in choirs offer numerous opportunities to cultivate new friendships at university and even in our working lives. Playing regularly in an orchestra will at the very least ensure your daughter's ongoing musical and technical progress.

It is also important that your daughter's violin repertoire is not constantly driven by exams. Ask your daughter's music teacher to introduce a more varied repertoire, including lighter, contemporary music, if he or she is not already doing so. There is a plethora of repertoire published and readily available, including some with backing tracks on CD. Even though this might not be for the purist, such repertoire provides hours of playing pleasure for the young instrumentalist.

There is so much evidence to support the fact that the discipline of learning to play an instrument encourages greater levels of concentration and learning in all other aspects of children's academic lives. It is also important to remember that playing a musical instrument helps to provide a breadth of experience, creating another avenue for our daughters to achieve success and grow in self-confidence. So, off with the excess pressure, applaud loudly at your daughter's concerts and enjoy her orchestral playing, find some fun repertoire and celebrate your daughter's success as a player at every opportunity!

My daughter doesn't contribute in class

Q: My daughter is a happy, chatty girl at home, but her teachers tell me that she is too quiet in class. Does this matter?

A: This is a common problem with teenage girls. Many are shy and self-conscious in front of teachers and classmates. They worry about getting things wrong and feeling embarrassed. This is a natural reaction and one that many girls experience, particularly as self-consciousness grows and peer approval becomes increasingly important. A good teacher will create a positive, supportive and encouraging environment in the classroom, making it easier for the girls to join in without fear of adverse reactions if they get something 'wrong'. This is crucial, as wrong answers are vital in the learning process. It is important to recognise that 'wrong' answers are usually far more interesting and informative than an immediate 'right' answer, as they allow for discussion and debate. Explain this to your daughter and try gently encouraging her to take risks in class. Perhaps suggest that she start by picking a subject about which she feels particularly comfortable with the teacher, and give herself the target of answering, or asking, at least one question during that lesson. Having a small, achievable target to start with can help girls to gain the confidence to spread their wings. Then they can set themselves the same target in other lessons, until eventually they can set themselves bigger targets, such as being prepared to lead a discussion group or present material in class. Gradually, they will be able to join in more effectively in more lessons, and will get a lot more out of them as a result. Joining in helps understanding, recall and enjoyment — so it's worth helping your daughter to conquer the fear.

Ages 16-18

The young woman your daughter has become will seem independent, and yet she still needs you. She has some significant decisions to make about her academic courses and future direction and she wants to be taken seriously. She will want you to relate to her as a fellow adult, and yet she remains your baby in many ways. Now that she is better able to relate to adults and to appreciate others' points of view, you will have some fascinating and occasionally challenging debates as she establishes herself as an independent young adult. She may be passionate about saving the world and may develop different social and political views from you. Enjoy the discussions, respect her opinions and ask her to respect yours.

16—18s — education choices

For most girls, this stage will pass very quickly. Your daughter should think carefully about where she wants to study for A level and what she wants to study. She may have a clear idea of a future career or, more likely, still be considering a wide range of alternatives. Encourage her to follow her interests, as she is more likely to do well in the subjects she enjoys, but also to choose a sensible 'package' of subjects. Currently, there is much debate over whether all A level subjects are equal in the eyes of future employers and universities. If your daughter is aiming to go to university, she should research which A levels are required for the courses she is interested in studying.

The A level course is divided into two separate but linked stages, AS and A2. In Year 12, most girls take four AS subjects. The AS qualification is gained through examination modules, of which there are usually two. The marks for each module are then aggregated, and a final mark that equates to a grade is achieved. At A2, most girls drop one subject and continue the other three. The

EDUCATING

221

system is the same as AS, but A2 modules are significantly more difficult, so it is important to 'bank' as many marks as possible at AS. For more information on A levels please see the Parents' guide – exams and qualifications on p262. The examination structure in Scotland is somewhat different. Please see Parents' guide – Scottish qualifications (p265) for further information.

During Year 12, most girls will be thinking about what to do after school, and certainly by the third term your daughter will be expected to start the process of applying to university or college. The key here is preparation and matching expectation to performance. Universities want the selection process to be fair and make their grade expectations very clear. Of course, it is possible to make dramatic progress in Year 13, but it does not happen often and schools have to make realistic predictions based on AS performance. A candidate with three Ds will not get offers for courses with an entry requirement of three Bs! Vocational courses, such as in art, fashion or drama, will require your daughter to have a portfolio, which her relevant teachers will help her prepare.

Candidates for medicine and law, in particular, may have to take specific aptitude tests – BioMedical Admissions Test (BMAT), National Admissions Test for Law (LNAT), etc., and Oxford, Cambridge and some other leading universities have some specific requirements and procedures for some subjects. Research and preparation are key to a successful application. Encourage your daughter to research her places of interest online and through paper prospectuses, and if she meets the entrance criteria, to go for it!

Your daughter will have to write a personal statement as part of the UCAS (University and College Application Scheme) form. This is a very important element but surprisingly difficult to get right – your help will be invaluable at this stage. Again, a lot of advice is available – use it and start the drafting process early. Schools will have their own deadlines based on the UCAS submission dates to ensure forms are completed and signed on time

– you will need to make sure you and your daughter are aware of these. There is also a parent section on the UCAS website www.ucas.com, which provides advice and guidance to parents on supporting your daughter through the application process and beyond. The important dates to remember are the following:

- Mid-October – last date for receipt of applications to Oxford, Cambridge, medicine, dentistry, veterinary science or veterinary medicine.
- Mid-January – deadline for applications from UK and EU students to be guaranteed equal academic consideration.
- Different arrangements apply for applications for art and design courses (B Route) and details are available on the UCAS website. Make sure to check these for any relevant dates.

A gap year can be an invaluable experience. Here, research, thought and care will be the keys to success. Universities do have a high regard for girls who have spent the year out wisely, done something that has challenged and developed them and been worthwhile, but you have to be prepared for the drain on your wallet and to make sure that the year does not become an extended holiday! Earning the necessary money to fund her trip should be an invaluable learning experience for your daughter and will show future employers that she is able to persevere to attain her goals.

Useful links:

Gap year – This directory provides everything you need to know if you are planning a gap year of work, travel or adventure: www.gapyeardirectory.co.uk

Lattitude Global Volunteering – a charity specialising in volunteering for 17–25-year-olds: www.lattitude.org.uk

EDUCATING

16—18s — development stages

In their autonomous years, girls take themselves very seriously. They take greater control of their own lives, making choices that will affect their future. Choice provides motivation, and girls become more reflective about their own learning, strengths and talents. The frontal lobe of girls' brains is the last area to develop, and this affects impulse control, judgment and problem-solving. As her brain and body continue to mature, she becomes less narcissistic than during the previous stage.

During this stage, parents become people; she can now understand your perspective, as well as those of others. Your daughter should be socially confident and able to relate well to adults on an adult-to-adult basis. Although she is finding her own voice, she still wants you to listen to and be interested in her and to be proud of and respect who she is becoming. You can help her to see the truth about who she is beyond simply what she looks like.

Many girls have not yet made decisions about their future career. Within schools and colleges, they will have more freedom and privileges, as well as opportunities for taking responsibility. As she develops her own values and ideals, your daughter needs you as an adviser and confidante: to reassure her, to act as a sounding board as she explores her thoughts and as the person who loves her, even when she gets things 'wrong'.

16—18s — tips for parents

- Keep listening to her and talking with, not at, her. She will be taking her friends' views more seriously than yours at times; after all, what can you possibly know about being a teenager! Her friends' opinions are vital to her self-confidence. Don't be tempted to criticise them too harshly, or she may stop listening to you.

- When she is making choices about her future, remember that the world she will live and work in is rapidly changing so your experiences may not be particularly relevant. Your job is to give her the confidence to make choices that are right for her.

- Not everyone will have a job for life. Many will change careers more than once. This means that a broad education is vital; help her to keep her options open by avoiding the pressure to specialise too soon. Encourage 'soft' skills, such as the ability to work in a team, to empathise and to express herself clearly.

- She will need lots of support from you as she starts sixth form. Boost her confidence, reassure her, help her to organise her work so that she meets deadlines and set house rules about how often she is allowed to go out during the week.

- A part-time job can help her to manage her money, organise her time and develop skills she will need in her adult life. It's all about balance; make sure she is still able to keep up with her academic studies.

- From now on, your relationship with your daughter is an advisory one and she may not always choose to take your advice. Try to avoid saying 'I told you so', even when you did! We all had to learn some things the hard way.

Moving into the sixth form

The sixth form today is more pressurised than when many of us were at school, with a constant stream of modular exams, modular re-sits, coursework and mock exams. There are also many other pressures on students, so it is vital that you keep the channels of communication open with your daughter.

Parents often worry about how to relate to their daughters at this age – how involved to be in their schooling and how much space to give them. Every family will find its own solution to

EDUCATING

this, but it is important to be aware of the expectations of your daughter's school or college so that you can help her to balance the sometimes conflicting priorities of academic study and a lively social life. A positive message is to work hard and play hard – in that order – so advise her to develop the habit of enjoying herself with the clear conscience that comes from being up to date with her work.

By setting out your stall like this, from day one, you will not have to nag her about getting enough sleep during the week or finding time to eat healthily. She will know your expectations and understand that you will cut her some slack at the weekends. It is far better to negotiate responsibilities and privileges in advance than to arrive at these arrangements piecemeal when she starts to challenge the boundaries.

Many schools will have an introduction to the sixth form or a separate induction programme. Make sure you get to these. If you can't, make an individual appointment to see your daughter's head of sixth form, so that you are up to speed with what the school or college expects on key issues: homework hours per subject; time spent on independent study; how study periods or 'free' time should be spent during the school day; dress code; driving lessons; permission to be off-site during the day and commitment to the extracurricular programme.

From your daughter's point of view, the sixth form is an exciting new phase in her life, linked in her mind with the sorts of freedoms that come with being older. It is a tricky job for parents not to burst that bubble, while at the same time driving home the message that these adult freedoms can only be enjoyed if students have adult attitudes to the responsibilities that accompany them. Preach the virtues of self-discipline and good organisation from day one: students who do well in the lower sixth (Year 12) are those who learn quickly to use their time wisely and to resist peer pressures to see school/college as primarily a social scene.

Be clear to her that the sixth form is a big step up from GCSE and that she shouldn't expect to be spoon-fed. Her AS exams will be the main results influencing predicted university grades and university offers. A miserable upper sixth year re-sitting AS modules, as well as studying for A2 exams, is simply too high a price to pay for drifting through the lower sixth. At the same time, be realistic about expectations, both yours and hers. You may have gone to Cambridge, but this may not be your daughter's dream or appropriate to her ability level. Encourage her to be her own person, identify her own strengths and work towards attainable goals.

For those starting at a different school, particularly if they are moving to a co-ed environment, the demands and social pressures of making new friends, learning new ways of doing things and becoming established with an unknown group of teachers may feel even greater. Make clear to her that the real challenge is not to 'dress to impress', but to hit the ground running, as those first AS modules may only be a few months away. Finding your bearings and a new social circle always takes time, and it doesn't pay to force the pace.

Above all, be there to listen to your daughter and to make sure that she sees you actively supporting the expectations of her school. Parents and teachers all want the same things and these can best be achieved by working closely together.

Settling into sixth form

Returning to school as members of Year 12 is an exciting time for most students. They have enjoyed the extended summer break, and most of them are still on a high after their successes at GCSE. However, they may feel a certain degree of apprehension on several levels.

First day jitters can be as simple as 'What do I wear?' or 'Where

EDUCATING

do I sit in the Common Room?' Feelings with which we can all empathise. However, after the euphoria of meeting up with friends and settling into a new form starts to wear off, deep-rooted anxieties begin to emerge. They may include concerns about coping with the demands of A level study, doubts about having chosen the right subjects, integrating into the sixth form and balancing social and academic life.

All these concerns are valid and should be taken seriously. The sixth form should be a wonderfully exciting time in a student's life, during which they're able to study the subjects they really enjoy, develop their leadership skills and mature intellectually and socially. All of this can be achieved if Year 12 is seen as a positive experience from day one and if all of the student's initial 'teething problems' are dealt with promptly and effectively.

Where possible, schools try to allay some of these concerns while the students are still in Year 11. They are invited into school for a morning after they have finished their GCSEs. They are made aware of the sixth form dress code and they listen to lively presentations by the Head and Deputy Head about life in the sixth form – especially the common room! They also pick which committees they wish to join and have an input into their form groups. This pre-emptive strike leaves many of them saying they want to start straight away!

It is commonplace in many schools that as part of the settling-in process, Year 12 pupils may be taken 'off timetable' during the first two days of term so that they can undergo an induction process. Girls may be encouraged to consider their goals and targets and how they can be achieved. This may include a visit to the local university to gain a snapshot of university life. By the end of their induction, students have a clear picture about sixth form life and what will be expected of them. Year 13 students also play an important role in making the Year 12 students feel welcome during these early days.

The team of experienced sixth form tutors plays a vital role in helping the students make the transition with ease. They may discuss issues such as time management, coping with stress and becoming independent learners. They also deal with their students' academic and pastoral concerns. It can be particularly daunting for any new student into the school, so the form tutor may allocate a 'buddy' to take her to lessons and to generally look after her for the first few weeks.

A level results day

Results day. Images of happy, smiling girls embracing one another as they clutch envelopes containing results that confirm their plans for the next three years or more. But that doesn't tell the whole story. For some, the day is fraught with anxiety, as that rosy future seems to collapse around them.

Generally, your daughter will fall into one of the following categories:

- got the results she needed and is accepted by her first choice
- just missed her required grades but is accepted by her first choice
- missed grades required by her first choice but is accepted by her second choice
- has not met the grade requirements of either of her choices and has no offer
- done considerably better than anticipated

Naturally you will want to support and guide your daughter at this key point in her career. However, it is important that she takes responsibility for sorting out her own future. Encourage her to read the helpful Q&A section, be a good listener and offer TLC or congratulations as appropriate!

But what if your daughter is left without a place? There are

EDUCATING

still options available to her. If she narrowly missed the grades she required, it might be worth considering either a priority or a normal re-mark. Her school should be able to advise you both on this. If all else fails, you should help her seek to turn what appears to be a negative into a positive. She should start planning to take a gap year and to improve her application. Judiciously selected retakes might help her to improve her grades and a carefully planned year out, which might include some relevant work experience or gaining further skills and experience, will make her application stronger.

It's easy to say at a time when she's feeling insecure and her friends are happy and she has to face both them and relatives, but realistically, ten years down the line, no one will care that she took an extra year to access the course she wanted to do. Indeed, there is something to be said for approaching a university course with a little greater experience and maturity behind you.

Whatever your daughter's fate on results day, may she have every success in the future.

A level results – advice and next steps

The results are coming in – will your daughter have done better than expected, or will she be disappointed? Whatever the outcome, you both need to be prepared for what actions to take next. Below are some scenarios your daughter may be facing.

Q: I've got the results I wanted and have been accepted by my first choice. Do I need to do anything?
A: There is nothing much to be done, apart from accepting congratulations and realising that all of your hard work has been rewarded. Check on UCAS Track that your first choice offer has become an unconditional firm offer – i.e. you have been accepted.

Q: I've just missed the required grades but have been told I've still been accepted by my first choice. How can I be sure?
A: This will either be confirmed on Track or may require an anxious wait before a phone call to the university (ideally by you) confirms the outcome.

Q: I've missed the grades for my first choice but have been accepted by my second choice. Do I have to accept?
A: In this case, it might still be worth phoning your first choice to check. They might be able to offer you a place on a similar course. If not, your insurance offer is guaranteed.

Q: I've missed the required grades for both of my choices and am without an offer. Help!
A: Don't panic. In some cases, your firm and/or insurance choices may not have reached a final decision, and you might face a frustrating wait until they do so. Start looking at other courses just in case. All may appear lost and you will certainly be in need of some TLC, but tens of thousands find a place each year through the clearing process. Nevertheless, it will still be worth phoning both of your choices to see whether they can offer you a place on a course you would consider.

If not, it is a case of checking vacancies on Track, the UCAS website or in the *Independent* newspaper. You will need to be patient – UCAS and the universities receive tens of thousands of calls on results day alone. You do not have to – and should not necessarily – accept the first course you are offered. Universities are interested in filling vacancies. You need to be sure it is a course you are actually going to be happy on for three years or longer. Get advice from your school and check course details carefully. Keep a careful record of whom you spoke to and what was agreed.

Q: I've done considerably better than anticipated, and my grades have exceeded expectations. What should I do?

EDUCATING

A: You may want to reconsider your plans. In 2009, for the first time, UCAS introduced an 'adjustment week', designed to enable applicants like you who have exceeded expectations to hold on to their guaranteed offer while approaching other universities to see if they can find a place on a course requiring the higher grades they have achieved. It has not been in place long enough to know how well this will work in practice, and it appears unlikely that there will be many, if any, vacancies on more competitive courses.

16—18s — education Q&A

Results day — your questions answered
Q: My daughter has secured her first-choice offer, but she is now questioning whether the course is actually for her. She chose the course without considering a future career and now doesn't want to start a degree with no prospects. If she cancelled her offer, could she go through clearing for another course or would this put off potential universities? Would it be to her advantage to take a year out and apply again in the autumn?

A: Because you don't say what her course is or which university you are referring to, it is a little tricky to advise. She shouldn't rule out the place she has purely on the assumption that her chosen course offers no career prospects. Traditionally, the purpose of university is to study something for its own sake and to develop one's intellect. Employers are looking for people with fine minds; who are independent learners; who are lucid, able to work independently and are creative. These attributes come from many degree courses. If, on the other hand, she is no longer excited by the course, then she should withdraw. Due to funding cuts, places at good universities through clearing are now in short supply, so she might be wise to take a year out, work out what she really wants to do and reapply. Don't worry too much about how universities will view her as long as she can make a strong case for the course she finally applies to study. The last thing universities want is people who lack commitment.

Ages 18+

Your daughter may still ask for your advice, although she may not take it. Hopefully, you will have given her the domestic and financial knowledge and skills she needs at this stage, but be prepared for the fact that she will make mistakes on her route to full independence. Often the best learning comes from taking risks and occasionally failing. She still needs your approval – perhaps more now than at any time since her childhood. The reality of preparing to leave home (or not) is daunting to even the most confident-seeming girl. Make sure she knows how much you love her and how proud you are of her; you will always be the most important influence in her life, even if she does not acknowledge it.

18+ — education choices

If you compare your own career path with your daughter's post-university plans, one of the main differences you will see is the amount of choice today. This is not only because there are now careers not even invented when you were young, but also because there are now so many more acceptable routes.

Some girls will have a clear idea of their career path once they leave higher education. Some will have followed vocational courses that will lead them directly to the workplace. Others may have developed ideas while studying non-vocational degrees. Internships during university holidays can help to firm up plans. Some girls may still have no idea what they would like to do, and this can be mystifying, worrying and frustrating for their parents (as well as for the girls themselves).

It may be reassuring to know that all of the following are common, and even acceptable, to future employers:

* post-university gap years

- a further qualification that is academic rather than vocational
- a vocational course
- a company graduate-training programme
- direct entry into a job

Be prepared for intense competition for certain jobs; it may take a while for your daughter to secure the position she really wants.

Some girls will take a while to settle down into a particular career. It is predicted that young people will have a number of changes of career during their working lives, so it is helpful to encourage her flexibility, as well as the development of transfer-able skills.

It may be the last thing on her mind at the moment, but if, at some stage, your daughter wants to combine work with a family, and/or is very ambitious, then encourage her to check out how flexible companies (and even whole industries) are in enabling women to return to work successfully, and whether there are female role models within the hierarchy. As your daughter is researching or entering her career path, it is helpful for her to seek out established women already in her chosen industry to help her to start her path and to give her realistic advice on the industry as a whole, as well as any helpful tips for starting out.

18+ — development stages

Beyond sixth form, your daughter may leave home to go to college and may be living independently for part of the year. Hopefully, you will have helped her to prepare for this exciting but daunting stage. Most girls are excited about this next step but will still welcome your practical help and emotional

EDUCATING

235

reassurance. With your help, your daughter should have acquired the self-discipline she needs to make a successful transition.

She will probably still want to come home to her own room and will continue to want your praise and encouragement. Even at this age, girls can switch from competent young adult to needy child when life gets complicated. Unlike young teenagers, this age group is prepared to accept that parents might know best! Some girls experience difficulty adjusting to the extra independence. The more self-confidence and independence you can give her in her earlier years, the more likely it is that she will adapt successfully. Universities and colleges have advisory and support services to help your daughter if she has special physical, educational or emotional needs.

Your relationship with her will be increasingly one of equals, but she will always be your daughter.

18+ — tips for parents

- It's now 'hands-off' time. Unless your advice or help is directly requested, it's best not to interfere. She will need your practical support and help, but your task is to enable her to fly the nest. The best parenting results in a confident, competent child, not a dependent, needy one.
- Advice on financial management and awareness is vital, although when she gets it wrong, you should have a pre-prepared strategy. Decide to what extent you would be able or prepared to bail her out.
- Above all, she still needs to know that you love her. She will still want to come home to her own bedroom knowing she is always welcome, even with a term's worth of debt and washing in tow!

- She will need your help when things go wrong, but don't leap in – wait to be asked.
- When things do go wrong, she will probably call you and tell you just how dreadful everything is. She will then put down the phone and go on happily with her life, having dumped all her troubles on you! If you're worried, call her the next day to reassure yourself but don't be surprised if she's absolutely fine, while you have been awake all night worrying!
- Remember that a parent's role is life long and that you seldom get thanked at the time. Years later, she may let you know just how much she valued your loving support, but don't hold your breath. Your reward comes from the pride you feel in your delightful, talented, successful daughter.

Thoughts from a Head — why gap years are vital

Although the recession has affected the number of young people opting for this rite of passage, enthusiasm for taking a year out from studies to see the world prior to commencing university remains high.

Typically, a gap year works like this: the autumn is spent in some paid employment to save enough money to fund the travels and in making a university application if a deferred place was not secured in the upper sixth (Year 13). Come January, students embark on an enterprise overseas: volunteering in a centre for street children in Mombasa; working on a wildlife conservation project in Nicaragua; teaching English in a school in rural Ecuador. All these can be arranged, sometimes for a pretty hefty fee, through one of the multitude of gap year organisations that have sprung up in the last twenty years.

EDUCATING

Students usually commit between three and six months to volunteering, after which they are free to go travelling, with South-east Asia, Australia, New Zealand and South America currently among the most popular destinations. Cynics may condemn gap years as the self-indulgent escapism of privileged Western youth but, for many, the months away are transformational.

It can be a sobering experience to work in parts of the world where many are trapped by poverty and lack of advanced schooling. Often gap students will have already undertaken voluntary work in their home communities, but the discovery that they can engage a class of thirty Peruvian children with next to no resources, or the knowledge that they have made a small but significant difference to the lives of a small village in Tanzania by helping to build a well and a community hall, gives a particular sense of wellbeing. Students have to fend for themselves, make decisions and cope with discomfort and the occasional crisis – all for the first time, in most cases.

It is the paradox of our risk-averse age – in which health and safety legislation has made childhood cautious rather than carefree – that the gap year provides young people with the much-needed chance to face some risks to test their resourcefulness and build their resilience. Even though the internet has made it much easier to stay in touch and seek help in a crisis, the full benefit of a gap year will only be accrued if students leave with the mindset that they must rely on themselves to cope and be independent.

The other vital attributes are a genuine cultural curiosity and the open-mindedness to respond to serendipity. It's important to stay in some uncomfortable hostels and to try some unfamiliar food; it's exhilarating to change your plans on the spur of the moment with the friends you have just made. For the mollycoddled, inflexible and insular, the journey is the toughest and, hence, the most beneficial. It's no wonder that employers recognise the benefit of gap years as much for their character-forming value as for their worthwhile volunteering.

And how about the parents? Letting your precious offspring go does not come easily to this generation of nurturing parents, whom the state has encouraged to continually assess and reduce risk and to challenge any shortfall in child protection.

The occasional gap year tragedy only serves to fuel parental anxieties and to make that parting at Heathrow the start of months of sleepless nights. However, this can be reduced (although not decimated completely) if parents try to adopt the right mindset.

Anxiety is a perfectly natural emotion, but in the weeks preceding departure, it should be channelled towards sensible discussions about practical matters, such as managing money, health and insurance. In fact, most gap students are impressively well planned for their travels and have gleaned a lot of intelligence from those who have preceded them on their trail.

Thereafter, it's about trusting and letting go and, like other phases of parenting, resisting the urge to bail your child out if there is a glitch or to organise from a distance, however counter-intuitive this feels. The self-denial will be worth the gain when the returning gap traveller is more mature, less self-absorbed and attention-seeking, more outward-facing and considerate, more appreciative of her good fortune, happier in her own skin, with a confidence that comes from successfully dealing with adversity.

Today's 19-year-olds will spend a long time working, some say until they are 70. Before they take on the responsibilities of building their multiple careers, of mortgage and of children, the opportunity to experience freedom in the form of a gap year is easy to justify. If the voyage is also allowed to be one of self-discovery, then it is certainly well worth advocating.

Heads' tips — exam time

How to help your daughter – tips for exam time:

- Start revision in good time. Help her to write a clearly structured revision plan that includes time out, treats, fresh air and exercise. Ensure she knows she won't perform to her best if she's exhausted.

- Check your daughter's revision by focusing in on the subjects she is weak in. Many girls will start with their best subjects and leave the weak ones till the end.

- Use Post-its. Try different-coloured ones as reminders about vocabulary, formulae, quotes, etc. Display them on mirrors, doors or around computer screens.

- If she is stuck or seems bored, encourage her to use a different method of explaining, i.e. orally or in pictures/diagrams rather than writing more notes. Employing different methods uses different parts of the brain.

- Remind her to seek help/clarification from her teachers at school. Schools want to support your daughter, too!

- 'The way to eat an elephant is one bite at a time.' Get her to break revision into small chunks. It is better to do thirty minutes' successful revision than to plan five hours, feel overwhelmed and fail to start.

- Revision means looking over her work again. To move knowledge into long-term memory, your daughter needs to look at it at least five times.

- For external exams, remind her to read through all the exam questions and answers she has done in the last two years. This is very helpful short-term memory revision close to the exam.

- Ensure that she reads her exam timetable carefully and gets to the examination centre in good time. There is nothing worse than arriving flustered or entering the hall after the exam has started.

- Remind her of good examination technique: once in the exam room, read the questions and instructions carefully; what exactly is being asked? Be selective – just because you have learnt lots of information about a topic, don't throw it all in. Be precise, controlled and relevant. Make it easy for the examiner to reward you.

- Rather than banning her use of the computer and mobile, encourage her to negotiate a communication contract with her friends in which they agree which twenty minutes they will all go online/communicate with each other – and make her stick to it!
- Encourage your daughter to relax before bedtime so she sleeps long and well.

And some Heads' tips just for you:
- You know your daughter better than anyone. Does she need a push, or does she put herself under quite enough pressure and simply needs reassurance from you?
- Encourage her to do her best, especially if she is young, and then celebrate/treat her at the end of exams. That way she'll know you are really pleased with her for doing her best, regardless of her results. You can always celebrate again if her results are particularly good.
- Reassure your daughter that she should aim to be the best she can be but not to aim for perfection. You will love her whatever she achieves.
- Be prepared for the fact that your daughter will have suffered as no one has ever suffered before when preparing for the public examinations. Girls can tend to feel more pressure and anxiety than boys, and to get it all out of proportion. Reassure her, take as many pressures from her as possible and just be there to love and support her.
- Look after her really well – provide good meals, stock up on her favourite snacks, make her hot chocolate and encourage her to take breaks. On no account go away and leave your

daughter to look after herself – she needs to focus on her work and you need to look after her.

- She may be irritating during this period. Expect grumps and moans, high moments and lows, but bite your tongue. You're the adult.

- Be upbeat! Your daughter has enough stress of her own and cannot deal with your anxiety, too. Even if you feel desperately concerned that she is working too hard, or not working hard enough, you must avoid showing this worry. Your role is to be a bedrock of stability and optimism – she will be inspired by you if you do.

- And when she has driven you to your limits, take a deep breath, relax your shoulders and have a glass of wine!

Heads' tips — homework

Timing of homework:
- Try to encourage a regular routine for homework that includes where your daughter does her homework as well as at what time (before tea, after tea, etc.). Having a rhythm to study is important.

- Wherever possible, encourage your daughter to do her homework on the night it is set – especially for the younger ones. That way homework doesn't build up and it is less easy to forget it!

- Young people can find it hard to settle down to learn something on the night it is set when they know it won't be tested for a few days. Difficult though it is, encourage your daughter to begin learning that night, and she will learn more effectively because the lesson will still be fresh in her mind.

- Don't allow your daughter to spend too long on her homework. Find out approximately how long homework should take, as girls have a tendency to take too long in their quest to get everything as perfect as possible. If a piece of home-work is causing real difficulty or is taking too long, stop your daughter and write in her homework diary or on the piece of homework itself that she spent x minutes (or x hours!) on it and that you have stopped her so she can go to bed.

- If your daughter routinely seems to be taking longer than the allocated time, agree with the teacher or tutor that she will change to another pen colour once she gets past the allotted time so the teacher can see if there is a problem with processing, reading, organising herself, etc.

- If the amount of time spent on homework is causing stress and worry, try checking subtly to see if she is focusing too much on how it is presented, rather than on the content itself. While presentation is important, some girls can spend too long on illustrations, graphics and beautifully coloured print-outs.

- As girls move into senior school, you may see your daughter struggle with juggling pieces of homework that are set one day for handing in the following week, rather than on the next day. Help her to devise a schedule.

Organisation of homework:
- Be aware of your daughter's homework timetable and make sure you both refer to it regularly.

- Suggest she has a wall planner. Encourage her to keep a record of work set and deadline dates (especially good for course-work/controlled assessment). To boost her confidence, she could also record any good marks awarded. It's good for planning out-of-school activities as well!

- A key skill for secondary school pupils to master early on is the good management of books, equipment and personal belongings. Keep a watchful eye on the way your daughter cares for and organises these things, particularly if she tends to lose or forget to bring home the books or materials needed to complete the task set.

- For older children, buy them a set of brightly coloured box files and insist on a weekly bag sort to file away handouts and loose sheets. This avoids panic attacks when a key handout is missing just when it's needed for a piece of homework. It's quite staggering how many orphan sheets will collect over the course of a month or two. All can then be safely hole-punched or glued in the appropriate folder/exercise book. Encourage her to use the homework diary and coloured highlighters to annotate and distinguish homework for different subjects.

- Help and encourage your daughter to get the next day's books ready the evening before, to prevent arriving at school without the necessary book to be handed in.

- If your daughter's school uses homework diaries, look in it regularly to check that she is using it correctly and to see what work your daughter is doing.

Homework environments:

- Provide a good workspace – ideally away from distractions. Ensure good lighting, a good desk and chair, etc.

- Working on her own in a quiet bedroom may not be best for all girls – your daughter may feel more part of the household at the kitchen table, particularly when younger.

- Occasionally, listening to music while working can aid concentration. It is usually better if the music is without lyrics, as the spoken voice is distracting. However, if your daughter routinely listens to music while working, remind her that, before sitting exams, she needs to practise working in silence: there is no music allowed in the exam hall, so her brain needs to be accustomed to working in silence.

- Discourage television and radio during homework times. It is not possible to complete work quickly or effectively while watching TV or listening to a radio programme. TV time may then be a reward for homework completed – perhaps a programme that was recorded while she was working. This works much better than 'I'll do it after "x programme".' Technology can really help here in managing things.
- Consider banning mobile phones/social networking sites, etc. during homework times.
- Students will all insist that they need a computer to do their homework, and frequently they do, but this should be in a communal area. You can then check what screen she is looking at from time to time to ensure that she does not log on to a social networking site until her homework is finished. Even a bleep to alert them to a Facebook status update will cause distraction and, with the best will in the world, it will take a good ten minutes to get back to the concentration level they had before.

How you can help:
- By all means help your daughter, but don't do the work for her – and let the school know if you are having to help her frequently, as there may be an underlying problem that ought to be discussed.
- It is very hard to teach your own child, however gifted a teacher of other people's children you may be. It can set up huge tensions within the family and changes the dynamics. Better to get a friend to help and help their child in return!
- Although your natural parental instinct is to intervene and assist, especially in younger years, this may be very counter-productive. It is important for teachers to know whether the pupil has understood a concept, and your well-meaning assistance can muddy the waters. Girls need to understand the purpose of homework and realise that it is more important

to 'have a go' and discover what they can do, than to get it all correct with help. We need to teach girls that it is okay to take a risk at being wrong and fall short of perfection.

- Sometimes a teacher says 'spend twenty minutes on this', and the child insists that she will get into trouble if she does not complete the task. This should not be the case, but remember that twenty minutes spent working in front of the TV is not the same as twenty minutes' concentrated effort. Keep the channels of communication open with the child's tutor/form teacher to share any concerns.

- If your daughter's school issues homework diaries or time-tables, ensure that you check it regularly as it should detail what is expected of your daughter for her homework (provided she has used it effectively!), and checking it will reinforce to your daughter that it is a tool designed to help her organise herself. If used appropriately, it is a very efficient mode of communication between school and home.

- Take time to understand the mechanics of the homework system at your daughter's school in terms of when it is set, when it is due and so on. You need information, and some-times the information provided by your daughter might be confusing. The school can sometimes be a better source of accurate information than the child.

- Keep an eye on the levels of weekday after-school commit-ments and activities during term time. The school will expect that your daughter is able to do homework and if she has too many evening activities (or social events), she may become overwhelmed and fall behind.

- The best role you can play is helping her to make sure that this time is well spent: that she is 'working clever' as well as 'working hard'. By helping her to ensure concentration levels stay high and work is completed with minimum fuss and maximum impact, more time can be spent relaxing and enjoying life alongside achieving good academic outcomes.

EDUCATING

Heads' tips — summer reading

As the long summer holidays approach, one of the most important messages you can pass on to your daughter is to 'enjoy a good book'. It can be difficult to keep some girls reading, particularly during the teenage years. So rather than suggest they get lost in Austen or burrow into a Brontë (great books, though they are), let your daughter find her own level and set a good example by being found on your sunbed engrossed in a good book yourself! In addition, don't forget that many titles are available as audio books. These make a great diversion for long journeys, providing a welcome opportunity to share a story with the whole family, and you may find that your daughter will listen to her favourites again and again.

Below are some suggestions for contemporary books that you might want to share with your daughter. With the younger age groups, try to find time to read to or with her, and for the older age groups, you can recommend the titles below and just hope she lets you borrow them afterwards!

Ages 5–7:
The Great Nursery Rhyme Disaster, David Conway
Tom & the Dinosaur Egg, Ian Beck
That Rabbit Belongs to Emily Brown, Cressida Cowell
Rufferella, Vanessa Gill-Brown
Witch Baby & Me, Debbi Gliori
Oh, Kitty!, Bel Mooney
The Time-travelling Cat (series), Julia Jarman

Ages 7–11:
Madame Pamplemousse & Her Incredible Edibles,
    Rupert Kingfisher
Ingo, Helen Dunmore
Varjak Paw, S. F. Said

The Invention of Hugo Cabret, Brian Selznick
The White Giraffe, Lauren St John
Chronicles of Ancient Darkness (series), Michelle Paver
Red Sky in the Morning, Elizabeth Laird
The London Eye Mystery, Siobhan Dowd
Skulduggery Pleasant, Derek Landy
Ways to Live Forever, Sally Nicholls

Ages 11–15:
Everything on a Waffle, Polly Horvath
The Kiss of Death, Malcolm Rose
Running on the Cracks, Julia Donaldson
Deeper than Blue, Jill Hucklesby
The Carbon Diaries, 2015, Saci Lloyd
Stravaganza (quartet), Mary Hoffman
Rabbit-proof Fence, Doris Pilkington
Miles McGinty, Tom Gilling
Alis, Naomi Rich
The Red Necklace, Sally Gardner
Rowan the Strange, Julie Hearn
Girl, Missing, Sophie McKenzie
The Tales of the Otori (trilogy), Lian Hearn
The Knife of Never Letting Go, Patrick Ness
Ella Minnow Pea, Mark Dunn

Ages 15+:
The Boy in the Striped Pyjamas, John Boyne
Behind the Scenes at the Museum, Kate Atkinson
The Time Traveller's Wife, Audrey Niffenegger
The Kite Runner, Khaled Hosseini
The Book Thief, Markus Zusak
The Wave, Morton Rhue
Uncle Tungsten: Memories of a Chemical Boyhood, Oliver Sacks
Regeneration (trilogy), Pat Barker

249

Tamar, Mal Peet
Blood Red, Snow White, Marcus Sedgwick
Defiance, Nechama Tec
Before I Die, Jenny Downham

Heads' tips — summer reading: ideas for reluctant readers

In addition to the above main summer reading suggestions, here are some ideas for parents to help spur on reluctant readers or dyslexic children for whom reading is so important, but not always easy. Reluctant readers are put off by the size of the font, the spacing of the type and the thickness of the book. And all that before you even approach the story! As such, the story must have immediate impact and no difficult names and must be straightforward and easy to understand. Stories by Jacqueline Wilson, Roald Dahl and Dick King Smith may fulfil these criteria for various age groups.

In addition, any compilations of children's short stories are more enjoyable for those children (especially those with short-term memory challenges), as they can read and enjoy a single story in one sitting, then gradually extend the length of story as they gain more confidence. Try the following collections:

War: Stories of Conflict, edited by Michael Morpurgo
Tales from Earthsea, Ursula Le Guin
Short and Scary, Louise Cooper
Short! A Book of Very Short Stories, Kevin Crossley-Holland
Best of Friends, authors including Theresa Breslin and Robert Westall

For reluctant early teens, try books that are humorous, not too long and well laid out:

I Was a Teenage Worrier, Ros Asquith
Angels Unlimited (series), Annie Dalton

Diaries are another good source of short, sharp reading material. Try a factual approach, such as the *History Diaries* series, which features the daily thoughts and experiences of a teenager writing about his or her particular time and occupation or career; for example:

The Diary of a Young Elizabethan Actor
The Diary of a Young Nurse in World War II
The Diary of a 1960s Teenager
and many more . . .

Or try the trilogy of fictional diaries of a mother and teenage daughter by Yvonne Coppard:

Not Dressed Like that You Don't!
Everybody Else Does! Why Can't I?
Great, You've Just Ruined the Rest of my Life!

Finally, books on CD are an excellent idea. Dyslexic children are frequently frustrated by the material they can manage to read, and listening to audio books will enable them to 'read' books at the level at which they wish they were. Audio books also help to ensure that their vocabulary and comprehension are developed in a less stressful manner. Most public libraries lend books on CD as well as in printed form, so do take a look.

Above all, ensure that you and your daughter enjoy your summer reading!

Heads' tips — internet safety

The internet is an amazing tool, as well as an integral part of our children's lives, providing both new opportunities and new potential dangers. As a parent, you will want to equip your daughter with strategies for staying safe in the online world as much as you do in the real world. Here are our Heads' tips on staying safe online.

EDUCATING

Advice for parents:

- Try to keep any computer your daughter uses to access the internet out in the open, where anyone can see what is being written and communicated there, rather than tucked away in her bedroom. If your daughter objects, point out that if there is something being said that she feels uncomfortable sharing, then it is almost certainly questionable, if not necessarily absolutely wrong. Openness is one of the key ways to keep safe.
- Set up a family email address to use if your daughter wants to subscribe to any online services.
- Involve your children in writing your own family code of acceptable internet use. Remember that what's acceptable for a teenager isn't necessarily okay for a primary school-aged child, so get their input.
- Tell children not to give out their personal details. In particular, younger girls should be aware this does not just include telephone numbers and addresses, but also the name of their school, their intimate thoughts and feelings and, increasingly, pictures of themselves. Once information has been sent out in an email, by mobile phone or posted on a website, it can be easily copied, forwarded to others or amended, and you don't know where it will end up or who will get it.
- Encourage younger girls to memorise and follow the SMART rules at: www.kidsmart.org.uk/beingsmart.
- Be brave – limit the time you allow your daughter to spend on the computer.
- Talk to your daughter. Don't assume that everything is bad. Find out more before saying no.
- Always be honest and open with your daughter about potential dangers. You cannot protect her from the reality of risk, but you can educate her so that she is able to cope with it. If you are honest and open with her, she is more likely to be open and honest with you.

- Understand what your daughter is doing online. Get to know the internet and set up your own social networking account, so you have an idea about the perks and the pitfalls. If you aren't confident with computers, go on a course. This will allow you to have a more informed discussion with your daughter.
- Make sure that the security settings on home computers are appropriate and use your browser's controls, as some offer differing degrees of security for each family member.
- Invest in good internet filtering software. There are various parental controls on the market to restrict content, website addresses and even the time of day that the internet is accessible. Have a look at www.getnetwise.org for advice on what is available.
- The minimum age to have an account on a social networking site is 13. If someone younger than this has one, they have provided incorrect information on the sign-up page. Facebook will remove such accounts.
- Use Facebook yourself. Become your child's Facebook friend. If they won't accept you as a friend, encourage them to accept a different relative or close family friend. This helps everyone to keep in touch and people always think twice if they know that Granny can see what they are posting!
- Cyber-bullying – do not delete such messages. Save or print to have as evidence that cyber-bullying is taking place. Schools will want to deal with any bullying under their anti-bullying policy, even if it takes place away from the school site. Ideally, print out what is being said and give it to the appropriate member of staff.

Useful links
www.parentscentre.gov.uk
www.thinkuknow.co.uk
www.ceop.gov.uk

EDUCATING

www.chatdanger.com
www.childnet.com
www.kidsmart.org.uk/beingsmart

Advice for girls:

- The internet is a public place, not a private space. Remember not to post anything online that you would not want the world to know or see. Don't write anything in instant messenger, email or social networking sites that you wouldn't be happy to say face to face.

- Keep your password safe. Treat it like your toothbrush – never share it.

- Use a nickname online (not your real name) and a nickname that is not going to attract the wrong type of attention!

- Always have a good look at the privacy settings of any spaces where you post personal information and make sure you know who can see or copy your stuff!

- Get your friends and family to have a look at your spaces to check that you aren't giving out too much personal information or posting inappropriate photos/films, because they might see something you've missed.

- Look out for your friends online and do something if you think they are at risk.

- Treat your online space with respect – only allow your real life friends to link to you. If you haven't met them in real life, don't link to them.

- Beware: people might not be who they say they are, and their photos may not be real.

- If you are uncomfortable, upset or threatened by something you have seen or heard via the internet, remember that it's never too late to tell someone.

Heads' tips — parent-teacher evenings

Worried about what questions to ask at your next parent-teacher evening? Do you find you don't get as much out of the evening as you had hoped? Read our Heads' tips on how to make the most of this valuable opportunity.

Before the meeting:
- Do a little preparation beforehand: discuss with your daughter which subjects she feels happiest about; find out if there are any areas she is concerned about or positives she would like you to raise.
- Ask your daughter how she feels she is doing in each of her subjects in terms of the effort she puts in and how she believes she is progressing. By asking the same questions of the teachers, you will have information to compare and be able to identify any potential gaps.
- Remind your daughter that you don't like surprises, and that if there are any potential issues, you would prefer to hear about them from her initially.
- If you already know of a specific or potentially major problem or issue with your daughter, do not leave it until parent-teacher evening; ask for a separate meeting beforehand. These evenings are for relatively short, focused discussions, whereas issues requiring greater time and attention should be addressed through longer, specific and private meetings with relevant staff.
- Have a look at your daughter's homework diary or exercise books to see her recent work.
- Be ready with specific questions to ask the teacher; you will then get more out of your allotted time.

EDUCATING

255

Top tips:

- You should ask whatever you want to ask. If you don't know what a teacher means, do not feel embarrassed to ask; as a parent, you are not expected to have the specialist knowledge of every subject teacher.
- Take notes and ask staff for specific guidance that you can feed back to your daughter later.
- Be prepared to hear constructive criticism. While teachers will say good things (mostly), their job is to identify areas for improvement however big or small. Hearing negative things about your child can be difficult and upsetting, unless you are prepared.
- If you have your daughter with you, try not to tell her off in front of the teacher!
- Try not to impose your views about your own education on to your child, e.g. 'I hated Chemistry at school, so I don't expect that Molly will be any good at it.'
- Keep in mind that you are working in partnership with your daughter's teachers, with both parties wanting the same outcome. Smile – the evenings are designed to be constructive and positive for all!
- Teachers are always delighted to hear if your daughter is particularly enjoying their subject.

Questions you may want to ask:

- Are there any subjects my daughter is struggling with? What can I do to help?
- Is her progress in line with the expectations for the group/ class/school?
- What does she need to do in order to improve? How can I support her in this?
- What has she done well? What are her weaknesses in the subject? What can she do to address these?

- How does a grade A, B, etc. on her report relate to potential performance at GCSE/AS/A level?
- What grade should she be aiming to achieve in this subject? Is she on target to achieve this?
- How much time should my daughter spend on homework in this subject?
- Does she get on well with her peers? Her teachers?
- My teenager communicates in grunts. How can I know how well she is doing/progressing between reports/parent-teacher evenings?
- So what you are saying is . . . ?

After the meeting:
- Don't be afraid to ask for a subsequent meeting if you feel you haven't been able to deal with all your questions in the allotted time, or if you have further questions that arise later.
- If you really weren't able to make the meeting, ask the school to help arrange other times for you to meet your daughter's teachers.

Parents' guide — homework

What is homework for?

Homework assignments are usually set in order to consolidate or extend what your daughter has learnt during a lesson. They might include learning vocabulary or formulae; they might take the form of wider reading or further research; they might involve practising further or more complex examples to reinforce her understanding of a new topic. They should not be a series of 'finish off what we started in the lesson and did not complete'.

How do I know what homework my daughter should be doing?

As a parent, it is important for you to understand your daughter's school's policy on homework. Unless you know what she should be doing and why, you will not be able to support her. Most junior schools, or prep schools for girls up to the age of 11, will not set huge amounts of homework each evening. Usually, younger girls will have spellings to learn each week, reading to do, some maths to practise or times tables to learn and some writing for English or topic work. As your daughter becomes older, more homework will be expected from her, perhaps an hour or more each night in Year 7, increasing to up to two hours per night once she starts on her GCSE, AS and A level, IB or other advanced courses. Each subject she studies will have specific allocated time slots each week.

Most schools will issue parents with a homework timetable and a home-school diary for you to sign or write comments in. As your daughter enters adolescence, she may well become reluctant to share her diary with you or to let you see her homework. Try to show your interest without it becoming a battleground. Make sure that the school keeps you informed if your daughter is not completing her homework satisfactorily – it is too late to discover this from her end of year report.

How do I ensure that my daughter spends the right amount of time on her homework?

Girls can appear at both ends of the spectrum: those who spend far too long on their homework, never satisfied with their efforts, writing it up again, yet more neatly, and generally trying to make it perfect and those who spend as little time as possible on it and often deny its very existence. Girls from both these groups can also fall into the habit of not actually handing their work in to the right person or at the right time for marking.

Try to identify the best times for your daughter to do her homework. Often, girls benefit from a break and a rest when they return home from school, but if your daughter arrives home quite late because of sports or music activities, you need to ensure that she is not working too late at night and missing vital sleep. Schools will often allow girls to complete some of their homework in the library or a study room during the day, but don't fall into the trap of accepting, without checking, that your daughter has already finished all of her homework at school and can therefore spend the evening in front of the TV or computer or on the phone. Your daughter may claim that all homework has to be completed using a computer and will proceed to log on to social networking sites and chatrooms, while allegedly doing her homework. It is rare that a computer is needed for every subject, and it is a very good idea to restrict your daughter's access to social networking and chatroom sites. The same is true of telephone calls – no teacher sets homework that necessitates your daughter talking or texting on the phone to her close friends for hours on end! Homework necessitates an appropriate place, away from distractions, but still able to be monitored by you. It is true that music helps some girls to concentrate, but your daughter needs to show consideration to the rest of the family, so her music should not be too loud!

If your daughter is spending far too long on her homework, there may be two quite different reasons. One is that she is

EDUCATING

259

constantly distracted in the ways described above, so she is not actually concentrating on her work, but instead enjoying the social scene. The other reason is that she has perfectionist tendencies; in this case, it is important that she learns to recognise that homework can be 'good enough'. She must learn to stop and move on to the next piece of work.

How can I help my daughter with her homework?
Often you will not be able to help – or you will not be allowed to help! It won't benefit your daughter in the long run if someone else does her homework for her. However, you can offer to test her on spellings, vocabulary or times tables. But the best thing you can do is to offer her support and encouragement, provide a suitable study area, set clear guidelines for her as above and supply her with drinks and healthy snacks while she is working.

Parents' guide – diamond schools

The debate about single-sex vs. co-education is unlikely to be resolved. Young people behave differently when in single-sex and mixed company, and from this stem the different character and atmospheres that one finds in single-sex and co-educational schools. There are clear advantages to both approaches. On the one hand, single-sex classes seem to provide greater focus and allow young people the freedom to grow up at their own rate. On the other hand, some parents feel that segregating the sexes throughout the period of schooling is unnatural, when school is meant to be a preparation for life.

A 'diamond' structure combines both single-sex and co-educational teaching. Typically, boys and girls are taught together until the age of 11, then separately from 11–16, before coming back together again in a joint sixth form. Diamond schools are often the product of the merger of a boys' and girls' school, thus it is usual that at Key Stage 3 and 4 girls and boys can be taught separately on different sites. It is a common feature that boys and girls combine outside the classroom in activities such as academic trips and visits and in some co-curricular activities such as choirs, orchestras and the Duke of Edinburgh Award scheme.

Parents' guide — exams and qualifications

Acronyms are always confusing for those who do not speak the 'language', and education is one of the worst offenders in this respect. It can be most confusing for parents trying to understand the huge range of assessment procedures their daughters will be facing. Here is a short guide to the main types of examinations that lie ahead.

GCSE (General Certificate of Secondary Education):

These examinations are taken by the majority of students in the UK, usually in Years 10 and 11 (14–16-year-olds) – although some schools are now starting these in Year 9, particularly in science, where they can study core and additional science over three years. A key feature of the new GCSEs, which began in 2010 in most subjects, is the end of coursework, which has been instead replaced by 'controlled tests'. These, in simple terms, are supervised tasks within school, taken under examination conditions. Re-sits are possible since the specifications (syllabus) for GCSEs have become 'unitised', or divided into modules. The new GCSEs emphasise transferable skills as much as subject knowledge. They are graded from A* to G, but in order to progress to A levels, grades of

A* to C are normally required. Schools may also require that this includes English and maths, or set boundaries of A or A* in the subjects to be studied in the sixth form.

IGCSE (International General Certificate of Secondary Education)

This is an international qualification and has traditionally been taken by 14–16-year-old pupils in international schools abroad. It has become popular in independent schools in this country, as some schools believe that it better prepares students for A level, particularly in science and maths, as they have more knowledge at a higher level than GCSEs. IGCSEs are knowledge-based, narrower in scope and most do not have any coursework. There is no oral test in French or compulsory Shakespeare study in English Literature, for example. There are no modules, instead a final examination at the end of the two-year course. This makes them similar to the old O levels.

AS level (Advanced Subsidiary):

Studied in the first year of sixth form, when students are 16 to 17, these exams usually follow courses in four subjects. Introduced in 2000, the intention was to broaden the range of subjects studied. Most subjects have four modules, two studied in the lower sixth and two in the upper sixth, although a few subjects have six. Modules may be taken in January and June, with results in March and August, and they can be re-sat. It is the Uniform Mark Scale (UMS) that determines the final grade. The AS can be a stand-alone qualification and is worth half a full A level, or it can contribute 50 per cent towards the full A level. Most modules are assessed by examination, but some are assessed internally or as an element of coursework. There is an assessment of practical skills in the sciences, art, music and languages, for example. The AS level course covers the less demanding material covered in an A level course, and grades range from A to E if you decide not to continue the subject to the full A level.

A2 (Advanced 2):

This is the second half of the full A level, not a separate stand-alone qualification, and covers more demanding material. Students usually study three subjects at this level, dropping and certificating their weakest or least favourite AS subject. There is a synoptic element in A2, combining knowledge and understanding across the whole A level course. Revised A level specifications were introduced in September 2008, with a new A* grade awarded for the first time in 2010. To achieve an A*, students must have a grade A overall at A level and a score of over 90 per cent (180/200) in the two A2 modules. A*s are not awarded at AS level. From 2010, full A levels have been graded on an A* through E scale. A student would normally require five GCSEs at grades A* through C and at least two A levels, or equivalent, in order to progress to a university course. There are, in addition, a small number of vocational A levels, covering such areas as business, health and tourism, called Applied A levels.

EPQ (Extended Project Qualification):

This is part of the English examination boards' attempt to answer the criticism that A levels are too narrow. The format is like the IB extended essay – see below. Although still a new qualification, British universities are showing a great deal of interest in this. Combined with A levels, it leads to a diploma, sometimes called the English Baccalaureate.

IB (International Baccalaureate):

This is studied in the sixth form as a two-year course. Students study six subjects: normally three at standard level and three at higher level, selected from six subject groups comprising language, individuals and societies, mathematics and computer science, arts, experimental sciences and second language. In addition, there are three core requirements: an extended essay with a 4,000-word limit on any subject of the student's choice and requiring individual research; a theory of knowledge course, which is interdisciplinary and encourages an appreciation of other cultural perspectives, and a community-action requirement, in which students volunteer in sports and community work. Assessment is at the end of the two-year course and is a mixture of internal assessments by teachers and external examinations. The grading is arrived at by a points system, which equates to A level grades. IB is widely accepted by universities, but parents should note that it is necessary to be a good all-rounder to achieve the top points scores.

Cambridge Pre-U:

This is a new qualification, and the first teaching only started in September 2008. It is a two-year course with final examinations at the end. It was designed by a group of schools working with Cambridge University International Examinations board. The original design was to provide a more knowledge-based alternative to A levels without the structure of the IB. Cambridge Pre-U syllabi can be taken separately, are graded individually and can be mixed with A levels. Students study three principal subjects from a choice of twenty-six. They also complete an independent research project and follow a global perspectives course. A student could study two A levels and a Pre-U principal subject. These, along with the independent research project and global perspectives course, would form a Cambridge Pre-U diploma. For further information on other qualification types, see the list of sites at the back of this book.

Parents' guide — Scottish qualifications

Although the Scottish Qualifications Authority is planning to change qualifications from session 2013-2014, the following information will be applicable until that time.

Standard Grade

Standard Grade qualifications are equivalent to GCSE. They are designed to assess two year academic courses in a vast range of subjects (see SQA website www.sqa.org.uk). Standard Grades can be examined at two levels chosen from three (though Foundation is not available in some subjects):

Credit   (grades 1 and 2)
General   (grades 3 and 4)
Foundation   (grades 5 and 6)

A grade 7 may be awarded to any candidate who fails to reach the standard required in the examinations, but who has completed all elements of the course. Most candidates attempt Credit and General levels, and, for the purpose of employers, a grade 3 or above is considered the equivalent of an old O grade or O level pass. Many universities specify as a requirement a Credit grade in mathematics for admission to a course like Primary Teaching.

Intermediate 1 and Intermediate 2

Originally designed as fifth year qualifications for those who were not ready to take Higher courses, these qualifications are often preferred to Standard Grades because in some subjects they are regarded as being a better preparation for Higher examinations. Since this view does not prevail for all subjects, it has become the practice for secondary schools to offer a combination of Standard Grade and Intermediate courses, depending on the preference of curriculum leaders. Intermediate passes are awarded at A, B, C (or D), with A, B and C passes being equivalent to the old O

EDUCATING

grade or O level qualifications. Grade A at Intermediate 2 attracts a few more UCAS points than Standard Grade Credit 1, but is of roughly equal value. Intermediate 1 may lead on to Intermediate 2. Both qualifications require the candidate to pass internally assessed NAB (National Assessment Bank) assessments, pertinent to discrete units of the courses, before the external examination qualification can be awarded. These NABs are subject to external moderation, and each year most schools have to submit a sample of pupils' assessments in subjects selected by the SQA.

Access Courses

Access courses are also offered in some schools (at three levels) for those students for whom Intermediate 1 would be too demanding. These courses are internally assessed and they are sometimes offered in schools as 'taster' courses for practical subjects like food technology or photography. In many subjects Access 3 is awarded to Intermediate 1 candidates who successfully complete the internal assessments but fail to achieve an award in the final examination.

Higher

Higher qualifications remain the 'Gold Standard' for admission to many Scottish universities, and students with five A grade passes might reasonably expect unconditional offers for admission even to courses like Medicine and Law at top Scottish universities (provided other expectations, like UKCAT, LNAT or work experience, etc are also met). Some English universities also give unconditional offers on the basis of Higher results (but see Advanced Higher below).

Pass grades are usually considered to be at A (bands 1 and band 2), B (bands 3 and 4) and C (bands 5 and 6), though D (band 7) may also be awarded. The minimum standard offer for some university courses is CCC. Able candidates usually take five Higher courses concurrently, and each Higher qualification attracts more UCAS points than the (roughly equivalent) AS course in England and Wales.

No external award can be given unless an examination candidate has also passed internally assessed NABs (as for Intermediate 1 and 2).

Advanced Higher

The Advanced Higher replaced the CSYS qualification about ten years ago. It has grown in popularity and currency throughout the UK's universities because it is regarded as a rigorous qualification and an excellent introduction to university courses. Some Scottish universities admit candidates with good Advanced Higher results into the second year of their university courses (though the take-up of such offers is small).

Although the Advanced Higher used to attract the same UCAS points allocation, grade for grade, as an A level qualification, since 2009 the Advanced Higher grades have been allocated more. There is no A* equivalent, however. The grading for Advanced Higher external assessments follows the same pattern as that of Highers and Intermediate examinations. NABs are also a feature of this qualification (see above).

Advanced Higher courses characteristically include a dissertation, project or investigation, which is allocated about a third of the total marks for the qualification. This element of original work, often involving considerable research, provides a bridge between school and university level work.

The Scottish Baccalaureate

This group award is available to sixth year students who combine study at Advanced Higher with an extended project, linking languages or sciences to the world of work. Highers can also be taken into account. The Scottish Baccalaureate was first introduced during session 2009-2010 and take-up has been small so far. Only two Advanced Highers, in combination with specified

EDUCATING

Higher qualifications and the extended project, are necessary for the award of the Baccalaureate. The Scottish Baccalaureate has not yet formed part of any university admissions requirement. It can be awarded 'with distinction'.

Future developments

It is anticipated that students currently (2010-2011) in the first year of secondary school will be taking courses leading to new qualifications (National 4 and National 5) at the end of session 2013-2014. These new qualifications will replace Standard Grade and Intermediate 1 and 2 qualifications. Highers and Advanced Highers (as well as Access courses) will remain but will be subject to some revision over the course of the next five to six years.

Parents' guide — interpreting league tables

School league tables have been with us for over fifteen years. But do they actually tell you which schools are best, and how much should they influence you when it comes to choosing a school for your daughter? In isolation, a league table of one year of A level or GCSE results simply tells you how each school fared that year with that particular group of students and in relation to other schools. It sounds simple, but here are some of the issues you need to bear in mind when looking at them.

Measuring different things

A major problem for parents is the sheer number of school league tables that are in existence. Broadly, they fall into two categories: those produced by national and local newspapers and those produced by the government, usually each January. Newspapers publish league tables based on GCSE and A level exam results each summer from data usually supplied to them directly by schools or, in the case of independent schools, by the Independent Schools Council. The earlier the tables are produced following the publication of the exam results, the less accurate they are likely to be, as they fail to take into account any re-marks or missing grades that frequently occur each year. Each newspaper will decide how it wishes to rank the exam results, and this is why a school can appear in completely different positions in different league tables. For instance, some newspapers will count the quantity of exams taken, giving points for each grade awarded, whereas others will focus on quality, ranking schools according to percentages of top grades. This means that schools with a policy of entering its students for no more than, say, eight GCSEs might be penalised, whereas a school that allows students to take as many GCSEs as they like may be favoured. This does not mean that the first school is any less successful than the second; it is merely a reflection of that school's exams policy. Similarly, some newspapers will include General Studies at A level and others will not. As a general rule, the key statistic to focus on is the percentage of A* to B grades at A level and percentage of A and A* grades at GCSE.

Alternative qualifications

This issue is further clouded by the fact that many schools now adopt alternative qualifications to GCSE and A level. Qualifications such as the IGCSE, Pre-U and IB, which are now offered by an increasing number of schools, use different grading systems and cannot easily be translated into GCSE and A level equivalents.

How academically selective is the school?

The tables tell you how good the teaching is, up to a point. But, as critics will argue, the reader can only speculate on how much value the school has added. A school's league table position often tells you more about its admissions policy and how academically selective it is than how much value it gives to its students. You

EDUCATING

269

may not be choosing a highly academic school for your daughter, in which case a league table position is less of an indicator of that school's worth and may not give an accurate picture of the quality of the school.

The success of single-sex schools
Despite their shortcomings, league tables have demonstrated the academic success of single-sex schools. Such schools have dominated the tables since their inception, despite the fact that many of them are not highly academically selective.

Future of league tables
Many educationists now feel that the days of league tables are numbered. With many schools diversifying into different exams, it is getting harder to make any credible comparison. Many Heads in the independent sector feel that league tables give an inaccurate and misleading picture of the worth of their school and have stopped submitting their results.

In reality, what matters most is not whether a school had a good year and crept up a few places in the tables, but whether the school's performance is consistent over the years. What you want to know is that, if you choose a school for your daughter, you can be confident that the staff and systems are in place to allow her to flourish.

Appendix 1 – Girls' Schools Association member schools

Bath
The Royal High School Bath GDST — www.royalhighbath.co.uk

Bedfordshire
Bedford High School — www.bedfordhigh.co.uk
Dame Alice Harpur School — www.dahs.co.uk
St Andrew's School — www.standrewsschoolbedford.com

Berkshire
Downe House — www.downehouse.net
Heathfield School — www.heathfieldstmarys.net
Luckley-Oakfield School — www.luckley.wokingham.sch.uk
Queen Anne's School Caversham — www.qas.org.uk
St Gabriel's School — www.stgabriels.co.uk
St George's School Ascot — www.stgeorges-ascot.org.uk
St Mary's School Ascot — www.st-marys-ascot.co.uk
The Abbey School — www.theabbey.co.uk
The Brigidine School — www.brigidine.org.uk
The Marist Senior School — www.themaristschools.com

Bristol
Badminton School — www.badminton.bristol.sch.uk
Redland High School for Girls — www.redlandhigh.com
The Red Maids' School — www.redmaids.bristol.sch.uk

Buckinghamshire
Pipers Corner School — www.piperscorner.co.uk
St Mary's School Gerrards Cross — www.stmarysschool.co.uk

Thornton College	www.thorntoncollege.com
Wycombe Abbey School	www.wycombeabbey.com

Cambridgeshire

St Mary's School Cambridge	www.stmaryscambridge.co.uk
The Stephen Perse Foundation	www.persegirls.com

Channel Isles

The Ladies' College	www.ladiescollege.sch.gg

Cheshire

Alderley Edge School for Girls	www.aesg.info
The Queen's School Chester	www.queens.cheshire.sch.uk

Cornwall

Truro High School for Girls	www.trurohigh.co.uk

County Durham

Durham High School for Girls	www.dhsfg.org.uk
Polam Hall School	www.polamhall.com

Derbyshire

Derby High School	www.derbyhigh.derby.sch.uk
Ockbrook School	www.ockbrook.derby.sch.uk

Devon

St Margaret's School (Exeter)	www.stmargarets-school.co.uk
Stover School	www.stover.co.uk
The Maynard School	www.maynard.co.uk

Dorset

Leweston School www.leweston.co.uk
Sherborne Girls www.sherborne.com
St Mary's School Shaftesbury www.st-marys-shaftesbury.co.uk
Talbot Heath School www.talbotheath.org.uk

East Sussex

Brighton & Hove www.bhhs.net
  High School GDST
Moira House Girls' School www.moirahouse.co.uk
Roedean School www.roedean.co.uk
St Leonards-Mayfield School www.mayfieldgirls.org

Essex

New Hall School www.newhallschool.co.uk
St Mary's School Colchester www.stmaryscolchester.org.uk

Gloucestershire

The Cheltenham Ladies' www.cheltladiescollege.org
  College
Westonbirt School www.westonbirt.gloucs.sch.uk

Hampshire

Farnborough Hill www.farnborough-hill.org.uk
Portsmouth High School www.portsmouthhigh.co.uk
  GDST
St Nicholas' School www.st-nicholas.hants.sch.uk
St Swithun's School www.stswithuns.com
Wykeham House School www.wykehamhouse.com

Hertfordshire

Abbot's Hill School www.abbotshill.herts.sch.uk
Berkhamsted School www.berkhamstedschool.org
Queenswood www.queenswood.org

Royal Masonic School for Girls	www.royalmasonic.herts.sch.uk
St Albans High School	www.stahs.org.uk
St Francis' College	www.st-francis.herts.sch.uk
St Margaret's School Bushey	www.stmargaretsbushy.org.uk
St Martha's Senior School	www.st-marthas.org.uk
The Haberdashers' Aske's School for Girls	www.habsgirls.org.uk
The Princess Helena College	www.princesshelenacollege.co.uk

Kent

Benenden School	www.benenden.kent.sch.uk
Bromley High School GDST	www.bromleyhigh.gdst.net
Cobham Hall	www.cobhamhall.com
Combe Bank School	www.combebank.kent.sch.uk
Kent College	www.kent-college.co.uk
Walthamstow Hall	www.walthamstow-hall.co.uk

Lancashire

Bolton School (Girls' Division)	www.boltonschool.com
Bury Grammar School Girls	www.bgsg.bury.sch.uk
Casterton School	www.castertonschool.co.uk
Westholme School	www.westholmeschool.com

Leicestershire

| Leicester High School for Girls | www.leicesterhigh.co.uk |
| Loughborough High School | www.leshigh.org |

Lincolnshire

| The Stamford Endowed Schools | www.ses.lincs.sch.uk |

London

Blackheath High School GDST	www.blackheathhighschool.gdst.net
Channing School	www.channing.co.uk
City of London School for Girls	www.clsg.org.uk
Francis Holland Sch (Regent's Park)	www.francisholland.org.uk
Francis Holland Sch (Sloane Square)	www.fhs-sw1.org.uk
James Allen's Girls' School	www.jags.org.uk
More House School	www.morehouse.org.uk
North London Collegiate School	www.nlcs.org.uk
Notting Hill & Ealing High School GDST	www.nhehs.gdst.net
Palmers Green High School	www.pghs.co.uk
Putney High School GDST	www.putneyhigh.gdst.net
Queen's College London	www.qcl.org.uk
Queen's Gate School	www.queensgate.org.uk
South Hampstead High School GDST	www.shhs.gdst.net
St James Senior Girls' School	www.stjamesgirls.co.uk
St Margaret's School, Hampstead	www.st-margarets.co.uk
St Paul's Girls' School	www.spgs.org
Streatham & Clapham High School GDST	www.schs.gdst.net
Sydenham High School GDST	www.sydenhamhighschool.gdst.net
The Godolphin and Latymer School	www.godolphinandlatymer.com
The Mount School (London)	www.mountschool.com

| The Royal School Hampstead | www.royalschoolhampstead.net |
| Wimbledon High School GDST | www.wimbledonhigh.gdst.net |

Manchester

| Manchester High School for Girls | www.manchesterhigh.co.uk |
| Withington Girls' School | www.withington.manchester.sch.uk |

Merseyside

| Merchant Taylors' Girls' School | www.merchanttaylors.com |

Middlesex

Heathfield School Pinner GDST	www.heathfield.gdst.net
Northwood College	www.northwoodcollege.co.uk
St Catherine's School Twickenham	www.stcatherineschool.co.uk
St Helen's School	www.sthn.co.uk
The Lady Eleanor Holles School	www.lehs.org.uk

Norfolk

| Hethersett Old Hall School | www.hohs.co.uk |
| Norwich High School GDST | www.norwichhigh.gdst.net |

North Yorkshire

Harrogate Ladies' College	www.hlc.org.uk
Queen Mary's School (Thirsk)	www.queenmarys.org
Teesside High School	www.teessidehigh.co.uk

Northamptonshire

Northampton High School
GDST — www.northamptonhigh.co.uk

Nottinghamshire

Hollygirt School — www.hollygirt.co.uk

Nottingham Girls' High
School GDST — www.nottinghamgirlshigh.gdst.net

Oxfordshire

Cranford House School — www.cranfordhouse.oxon.sch.uk

Oxford High School GDST — www.oxfordhigh.gdst.net

Rye St Antony School — www.ryestantony.co.uk

School of St Helen &
St Katharine — www.shsk.org.uk

Tudor Hall — www.tudorhallschool.com

Wychwood School — www.wychwoodschoolorg

Scotland

Craigholme School — www.craigholme.co.uk

Fernhill School — www.fernhillschool.co.uk

Kilgraston School — www.kilgraston.com

St George's School for Girls
(Edinburgh) — www.stgeorges-edin.sch.uk

St Margaret's School for
Girls (Aberdeen) — www.st-margaret.aberdeen.sch.uk

The Mary Erskine School — www.esms.edin.sch.uk

Shrewsbury

Shrewsbury High School
GDST — www.shrewsburyhigh.gdst.net

Shropshire
Moreton Hall   www.moretonhallschool.com

Somerset
Bruton School for Girls   www.brutonschool.co.uk

Staffordshire
Abbots Bromley School for Girls   www.abbotsbromley.staffs.sch.uk

St Dominic's High School for Girls   www.stdominicsschool.co.uk

St Dominic's Priory School   www.stdominicspriory.co.uk

Suffolk
Amberfield School   www.amberfield.suffolk.sch.uk

Ipswich High School GDST   www.ipswichhighschool.co.uk

Surrey
Croydon High School GDST   www.croydonhigh.gdst.net

Dunottar School   www.dunottar.surrey.sch.uk

Greenacre School for Girls   www.greenacre.surrey.sch.uk

Manor House School   www.manorhouseschool.org

Marymount International School   www.marymountlondon.com

Notre Dame Senior School   www.notredame.co.uk

Old Palace of John Whitgift School   www.oldpalaceof johnwhitgift.org

Prior's Field School   www.priorsfieldschool.com

Sir William Perkins's School   www.swps.org.uk

St Catherine's Bramley   www.stcatherines.info

St Teresa's School   www.stteresasschool.com

Sutton High School GDST   www.suttonhigh.gdst.net

The Royal School Haslemere   www.royal-school.org

Tormead School   www.tormeadschool.org.uk
Woldingham School   www.woldinghamschool.co.uk

South Yorkshire
Sheffield High School GDST   www.sheffieldhighschool.org.uk

Tyne & Wear
Central Newcastle High   www.newcastlehigh.gdst.net
    School GDST
Dame Allan's Girls' School   www.dameallans.co.uk
The Newcastle upon Tyne   www.churchhigh.com
    Church High School
Westfield School   www.westfield.newcastle.sch.uk

Wales
Haberdashers' Monmouth   www.habs-monmouth.org
    School for Girls
Howell's School (Denbigh)   www.howells.org
Howell's School, Llandaff   www.howells-cardiff.gdst.net
    GDST

Warwickshire
King's High School   www.kingshighwarwick.co.uk
The Kingsley School   www.thekingsleyschool.com

West Midlands
Edgbaston High School   www.edgbastonhigh.co.uk
    for Girls
Highclare School   www.highclareschool.co.uk
King Edward VI High   www.kehs.org.uk
    School for Girls
Saint Martin's   www.saintmartins-school.com

West Sussex

Burgess Hill School for Girls	www.burgesshill-school.com
Farlington School	www.farlingtonschool.net
Lavant House	www.lavanthouse.org.uk

West Yorkshire

Bradford Girls' Grammar School	www.bggs.com
Gateways School	www.gatewayschool.co.uk
The Grammar School at Leeds	www.gsal.org.uk
Wakefield Girls' High School	www.wgsf.org.uk

Wiltshire

St Mary's School Calne	www.stmaryscalne.org
Stonar School	www.stonarschool.com
The Godolphin School	www.godolphin.org

Worcestershire

Dodderhill School	www.dodderhill.co.uk
Malvern St James	www.malvernstjames.co.uk
St Mary's Girls' School	www.stmarys.org.uk

York

Queen Margaret's School (York)	www.queenmargarets.com
The Mount School (York)	www.mountschoolyork.co.uk

Affiliate Members

Colston's Girls' School	www.colstongirls.bristol.sch.uk
Lancaster Girls' Grammar School	www.lggs.org.uk
Leaden Hall School	www.leaden-hall.com
Stamford High School	www.ses.lincs.sch.uk
Ursuline Preparatory School	www.ursuline-prep.merton.sch.uk

Overseas Members

Canigo School	http://www.fomento.edu/canigo
Latifa School for Girls	www.lsg.sch.ae
San Silvestre School	www.sansilvestre.edu.pe
Unison World School	www.uws.edu.in
Westlake Girls' High School	www.westlakegirls.school.nz

Appendix 2 — Additional Contributors

Girlguiding UK – www.girlguiding.org.uk

Heather White, Adviser for PSHCE Education & Healthy Schools – Coventry City Council

Griselda Halling, Independent Nutrition – www.independent nutrition.co.uk

Sarah Anticoni, Family lawyer and Mediator – Charles Russell LLP

Imogen Vanderpump, Web Manager – www.MyDaughter.co.uk

Alison Morris, Editor – www.MyDaughter.co.uk

Reading list

Books and articles

Atwood, Margaret, *Cat's Eye* (Toronto: *McClelland & Stewart, 1988*)

Bean, Anita, *Healthy Eating for Kids* (London: A. & C. Black, 2004)

Green, Christopher, *New Toddler Taming,* revised edn (London: Vermilion, 2006)

Jardine, Cassandra, *How to be a Better Parent* (London: Vermilion, 2003)

Mellor, Ken and Elizabeth, *Teen Stages* (Warriewood, New South Wales: Finch Publishing, 2004)

Ward, Barbara and Associates, *Good Grief: Exploring Feelings, Loss and Death with Under Elevens, 2nd edn* (London and Philadelphia: *Jessica Kingsley, 1996)*

Websites

Bereavement

Child Bereavement Trust: www.childbereavement.org.uk

Cruse Bereavement Care: www.crusebereavementcare.org.uk

Winston's Wish: www.winstonswish.org.uk

Educating

Assessment and Qualifications Alliance (AQA): www.aqa.org.uk

Boarding Schools' Association: www.boarding.org.uk

Cambridge International Examinations Pre-U: www.cie.org.uk

Chatdanger: www.chatdanger.com

Child Exploitation and Online Protection Centre: www.ceop.gov.uk

Childnet International: www.childnet.com

Directgov: www.direct.gov.uk/

Edexcel: www.edexcel.com

Gap Year Directory: www.gapyeardirectory.co.uk

Independent Schools Council: www.isc.co.uk
International Baccalaureate (IB): www.ibo.org
Kidsmart: www.kidsmart.org.uk
Lattitude Global Volunteering: www.lattitude.org.uk
Montessori: www.montessori.org.uk
National Day Nurseries Association: www.ndna.org.uk
OCR: www.ocr.org.uk
Parents Centre: www.parentscentre.gov.uk
Scottish qualifications authority: www.sqa.org.uk
State Boarding Schools Association: www.sbsa.org.uk
Toe by Toe: www.toe-by-toe.co.uk
WJEC: www.wjec.co.uk

Food and diet
B-eat: www.b-eat.com
Foods Standards Agency: www.eatwell.gov.uk/agesandstages

Growing up
BBC: www.bbc.co.uk/parenting/childcare
Beating Addiction: www.beatingaddictions.co.uk
Breakthru Drug and Alcohol Awareness: www.breakthru.co.uk
Chatdanger: www.chatdanger.com
ChildLine: www.childline.org.uk
Counselling Directory: www.counselling-directory.org.uk
Directgov: www.parentscentre.gov.uk
Dove Self-Esteem Fund: www.campaignforrealbeauty.com
Embarrassing Problems.com: www.embarrassingproblems.com
Frank (drugs advice): www.talktofrank.com
KidSMART: www.kidsmart.org.uk/beingsmart
National Health Choices: www.nhs.uk/conditions/Body-piercing
NHS Clinical Knowledge Summaries: www.cks.nhs.uk
Parents Against Drug Abuse: www.pada.org.uk
Society for the Prevention of Solvent and Volatile Substance Abuse:
    www.re-solv.org

Think U Know: www.thinkuknow.co.uk

Val Besag, Bullying and Peer support: www.valbesag.co.uk

Relationships

Counselling Directory: www.counselling-directory.org.uk

Family Planning Association: www.fpa.org.uk

Gay and Lesbian Humanist Association: www.galha.org

GotATeenager (part of Parentlineplus): www.gotateenager.org.uk

Parentline Plus: www.parentlineplus.org.uk

Relate: www.relate.org.uk

Other useful sites

Child Protection UK Ltd: www.childprotectionukltd.co.uk

EU and Safer Internet Programme: www.saferinternet.org

Facebook: www.facebook.com/privacy/explanation.php.

Girls' Schools Association: www.gsa.uk.com

Mumsnet: www.Mumsnet.com.

My Daughter: www.MyDaughter.co.uk

National Childminding Association: www.ncma.org.uk

Index

Online advice for parents

Visit the site for more great articles, videos and tips from our experts.